A Doctor in XIVth Army

A Doctor in XIVth Army
Burma 1944–1945

by

CHARLES EVANS

With Illustrations by the Author

LEO COOPER
LONDON

First published in Great Britain in 1998 by
LEO COOPER

an imprint of
Pen & Sword Books Ltd
47 Church Street, Barnsley, South Yorkshire
S70 2AS

A CIP record for this book is available from the British Library

ISBN 0 85052 597 7

Typeset by Phoenix Typesetting, Ilkley, West Yorkshire
Printed in England by Redwood Books Ltd, Trowbridge, Wilts.

Contents

Foreword

Senior Officers did not much like us to talk of 'The Forgotten Army'; they thought it bad for morale. I liked the phrase; it was how men told you that they could put up with things. They knew that we were not much in the news and were low on lists of priorities, but they could laugh at all that, and they could carry on.

I kept a detailed diary during nearly all my short time in the army, and these notes are assembled from it. I have departed from the diary form where it would interrupt the narrative, but dates and places and events are all taken from the diary and from letters. Without them many of the details would have been forgotten. Conversations are as I wrote them down at the time, and comments about people and things are my own as written then in the heat of the moment. They often say more about me than about the subject of the comment.

Although I have used the official histories and other material to place the story in the general setting of the 1944/45 campaign in Burma, I must emphasize that the book is personal reminiscence, not an attempt at history. Some paragraphs, and some whole chapters, are printed in italics: they deal with the geographical and strategic background of my text and are intended to introduce the reader to the setting and circumstances of the story.

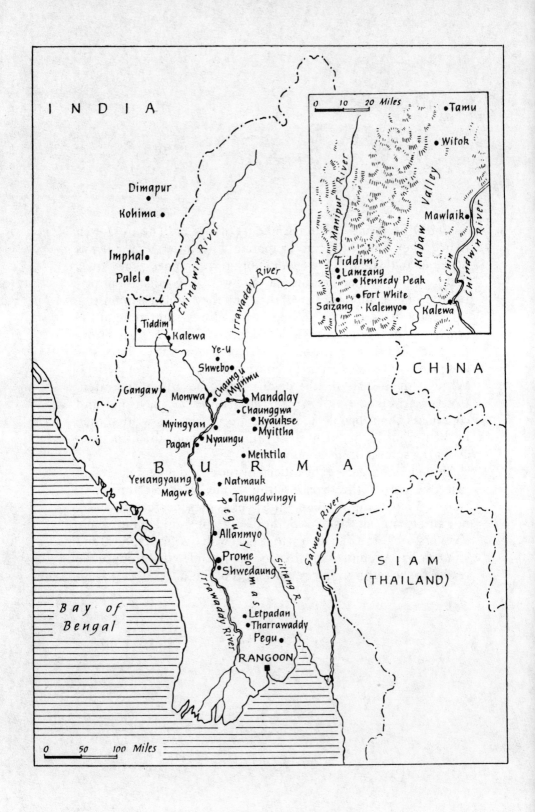

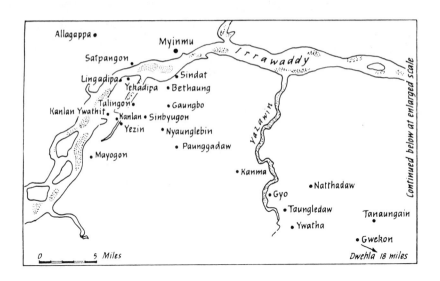

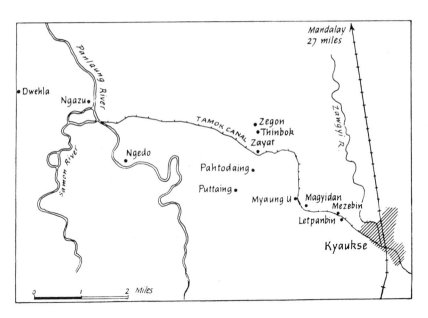

Chapter 1

Reserved Occupation

IN THE SUMMER of 1939 England was far from ready for war, but plans had at least been made to direct many people into work that would make use of their skills. Scientists, doctors, schoolmasters, farmers, miners and others who were needed to run the country found themselves in 'Reserved Occupations' and the muddle of an uncontrolled rush to join the forces, as happened in 1914, was avoided. It was all very sensible. The training of medical students was shortened, and if in the end they went into the Army, for example, they went as doctors, and not as recruits who for some time would not be useful soldiers. It was assumed that doctors, like others with a special trade, would have much to give. Like cooks and clergymen, mechanics and paymasters, they were needed to keep fighting men at the front.

When war came in September my return to university was delayed because of a mountain accident in North Wales in August and when I went back to Oxford in January, 1940, I found the place very different from the Oxford I had known. My friends who had not been doing medicine had left and were either already in the forces or waiting their turn to be called up. The colleges where we had lived were turned over to other uses and we lived that first winter of the war in Worcester College where I had a room in a part that seemed mediaeval. The small coal fire did not heat it; one window overlooked a quadrangle thinly dusted with snow; another overlooked the frozen pond and snow-covered lawns of the Fellows' Garden.

We ate our morning and evening meals in college; midday meals were taken at a sort of soup kitchen called a 'British Restaurant', a feature of that period of the war. We worked for long hours at the laboratories in Parks Road, in the libraries and later at the

Radcliffe Infirmary, but we felt frustrated at still being students and sought release for our energies in exercise arranged on the spur of the moment. When the pond in the Fellows' Garden at Worcester was frozen hard we found old skates and hockey sticks and played a game with no rules which we called 'Ice-hockey'. On other days when strong winds made the water rough on the open reaches of the Thames below Godstow we took to sailing the 'National' class dinghies of the University Sailing Club. Our outings on boisterous days did our discontented spirits a lot of good and usually ended in a capsize and a swim to the bank.

Then there were the girls. For me, brought up alone and taught at boys' schools, they were unknown and enticing, a world of human relationships to explore. The shortage of men and the plenty of young and attractive women then in Oxford were good for my education, and my memories of the ancient city are romantic and beautiful.

During the summer of 1940 we listened to every one of Winston Churchill's war broadcasts, to news of the overrunning of the Low Countries, the fall of France, the evacuation from Dunkirk and, above all, the Battle of Britain. When I try to recall my state of mind at this critical time in our history, I find it difficult to believe that with such knowledge of events as we were given I did not recognize invasion or defeat as real possibilities. We 'fire-watched' and played at being Home Guards, but I utterly failed, as I think did many of us, to recognize that real Germans with real tanks, rifles and bayonets might arrive in a matter of days on our country roads and in our Oxfordshire villages.

It was easy even then at Oxford to follow study and pleasure very much as one chose, careless of the world. I came easily under the spell of undergraduate life when I first went there. The lovely old buildings, the wide empty streets, and the rivers and meadows continued to delight me in the years that followed, and I grew to love the surrounding country and to make a habit of roaming over it whenever I was free. We walked the length of the Chilterns, wandered by day or night over the Cotswolds and the Berkshire Downs, and slept under the stars or under the beeches that grew in clumps on the tops. On these excursions I would only be brought back to wartime reality when a country policeman challenged me at night to show my identity card, or when, as I walked into Oxford by the Iffley Road, I saw over Cowley new Spitfires being thrown by test pilots into impossible dives and climbs.

Sterner reminders of war came after the invasion of France. One quiet sunny day I walked up by the Thames to Godstow. I was used to seeing across the river from the towpath the deserted expanse of Port Meadow where birds and a few grazing horses were as a rule the only signs of life. On this day there were men everywhere, standing about in small groups, brown, shirt-sleeved, in battle dress. Near each group small arms were stacked between bivouac tents, and cooking fires were lit: I was looking at survivors of Dunkirk. Back at the hospital more men from Dunkirk appeared; these were wounded Belgians who had fought their way back to the beaches and deeply resented King Leopold's recent capitulation to the Germans.

One incident over Oxford itself on a beautiful hot midsummer afternoon affected us all deeply. It was the sort of day which drew everyone out on the river and recalled for a moment the atmosphere of Oxford before the war; punts full of noisy, cheerful men and women passed up and down the Cherwell. We had tied our punt to the bank near Marsden Ferry and were lying in the grass gazing idly at a Wellington bomber which moved in level flight slowly across our sky. We suddenly saw the nose point down and the Wellington begin to dive. We watched without a sound, becoming aware, unbelievingly, that we were about to be in the presence of a disaster. No one was going to pull this aeroplane out of its dive into the middle of North Oxford. It disappeared in an orange flash surmounted by a great column of black smoke, and a dreadful quiet fell over the river.

Before 1939 there had only been five or six clinical students at the Radcliffe Infirmary. Oxford students, after the first three years, chose as a rule to go to one of the big London teaching hospitals. When war began those hospitals were themselves moved out into the country and arrangements for clinical teaching at Oxford were expanded to accommodate more than fifty students. The Radcliffe gained much as a teaching hospital by being in a university city and also close to a centre of manufacturing industry. Some university departments studied sciences allied to medicine, and the hospital's nearness to Morris Motors brought the benefactions of

Lord Nuffield and the creation of Nuffield departments of Medicine, Surgery, Anaesthetics, Obstetrics and Orthopaedics. The professors and their assistants in these specialized hospital departments gave an international standing to what was already a good small hospital and the amount and quality of teaching available at the Radcliffe was increased by the voluntary return from retirement of distinguished men such as Findlay from Glasgow, Gask from Bart's and Sir Arthur Hurst from Guy's, men by whom we should never otherwise have been taught.

There were also men from overseas, Trueta from Barcelona, with recent experience of the Spanish Civil War, and the two Guttmans, who were not related but were both refugees from Nazi Germany. Erich, who moved later to the Maudsley Hospital, taught me more psychiatry than I ever learnt from anyone else or from any book. Ludwig, who with his family used my mother's home in Wales for holidays, later became famous for his work at Stoke Mandeville. I remember him as a friendly martinet, obsessed by the effect of spinal injuries on sweating. He made us paint his patients with powders which changed colour when moist; then, with hot drinks and exposure to radiant heat, he made the patients sweat and photographed them. This helped to locate the site of the injury and earned him the nickname 'Sweaty Guttman'.

Men like Trueta and Cairns, the Nuffield Professor of surgery, great men in their own fields, were more than ready, if we were willing to listen, to share with us some of their wisdom. Trueta had experience unrivalled then of treating compound fractures in war and many bombing casualties which had had their primary treatment elsewhere came to him at the Radcliffe.

When we started as clinical students the medical world was on the threshold of discoveries and advances as a result of which many of the illnesses we were shown became almost extinct and operations which surgeons had not dared to contemplate became possible. Blood transfusion was then still at the 'jug and bottle' stage, far from ready for the demand for immediate blood transfusion that was to come with bombing and battle. If a patient needed blood someone of the same blood group, often a relative, was put into the next bed and bled into a jug; the blood in the jug was mixed with citrate to prevent clotting and poured into a glass bottle hanging from a stand at the foot of the patient's bed. From about that time blood in many thousands of bottles was stored all over the country in refrigerator 'banks'.

The most memorable work then going on at Oxford was Florey's development of penicillin for general use. Fleming had already discovered penicillin but it fell to Florey and Chain to find out how it worked and to make it available for clinical trial. A stage in the purification, we were told, was to feed the crude penicillin to the Oxford City Police from whose urine it was collected in purer form after passage through the body. If the story is true, then the policemen's contribution to human happiness was never adequately recognized. Now and then, as the work went on, Florey and Chain would call us in and tell us about it, so that later, when we were shown some of the early trials and witnessed the miracle of recovery that followed we could guess at the implications of what we saw. One patient was a man with an infection which had spread inside his head from a boil on the face, a condition up till then always fatal. Professor Gask drew our attention to the high fever, the swollen and discoloured features and the protruding eyes of the patient, now mercifully unconscious; he explained that as there was nothing to lose he was to be injected with large doses of the new drug. No one who was there during the next few days could ever forget the miracle of recovery that followed.

Cairns took the new drug to the battlefields of North Africa. He was by then a brigadier, running the Military Hospital for Head Injuries at St Hugh's College and ruling that despatch riders must for the first time wear crash helmets. He managed to visit his Neurosurgical Ward at the Radcliffe, lecture to students and find time to do long operations on tumours of the brain. I had a tempo-rary job at this time with his assistant, Joe Pennybacker, and 'The Chief' would sometimes surprise us in the ward, appearing in immaculate khaki, with the brigadier's crowns and stars set off by the sober ribbon of a recent decoration.

The opportunities at the Radcliffe were unrivalled and my only criticism of the teaching was that we did not become familiar enough with the 'common' illnesses that, according to an old saying among teachers in medical schools, 'are those which occur most often'. At the end of 1942 I passed my examinations and became a House Physician at the Radcliffe, working there for six months during what was probably the most momentous year of the war: the battle of the Atlantic reached its climax, Russia and America had become our allies, the whole of North Africa became ours, Sicily and Italy were invaded and in the Pacific the American fleet won the Battle of Midway. We did not know that these were turning points in the war and to us the future often seemed bleak; the beating of the Japanese in Burma and of the Germans in Europe were still two years away.

Any thoughts of staying longer at Oxford were dispelled by the arrival of my calling-up papers, and a very good thing too: I was becoming addicted to life as a hanger-on there. I was invited to put in an appearance on 4 September, 1943, at No. 1 Depot, RAMC Crookham, Hants. Here began a delightful six weeks during which we were told each minute of the day exactly where to go and what to do. We were lectured on the history, organization and administration of the RAMC and on how properly to conduct ourselves as officers, particularly with regard to dress. My completely passive role was pleasantly restful after the responsibilities of a job in a busy hospital and I loved the golden September days out of doors in the Hampshire countryside. I was in love at the time; Betty was a charmer whom I had got to know at Oxford, and by good fortune it was easy for us to meet while I was at Crookham. I set myself to learn Kipling's poem 'The Long Trail' by heart: it suited my mood and fitted in with my enjoyment of early autumn. When I read it now the vivid happiness of those English days floods back with memories of the contradictory feelings aroused on the one hand by love and on the other by the prospect of travel and adventure.

From Crookham we went for a week to the Army School of Hygiene at Mytchett. Hygiene, like Dietetics and Social Medicine, had always bored me, but I was pleased to find that at Mytchett we were taught practical things: how to build makeshift ovens in the open with stones and clay, how to cook over a flame produced by dropping a mixture of oil and water on a hot steel plate, the 'Oil and Water Splash Fire'. We were introduced to the 'Horrocks Box', the function of which was to show how much chlorine powder to add to water to make it safe to drink; it was invented by the father of the well-known general and historian, Sir

Brian Horrocks. The only tutor I remembered afterwards from our time at Mytchett was McKenny-Hughes, an entomologist disguised in the uniform of an Army major. He entertained us for hours with descriptions and demonstrations on stage of the disgusting life-style of the housefly.

There followed a crash course at the London School of Hygiene and Tropical Medicine where Professor Sir Philip Manson-Bahr taught us about malaria. He began his first lecture to us, 'Gentlemen, there are two sorts of Fevah: there is Fevah, and there is Damn Bad Fevah. Fevah is what you will get when you are living at Poonah, but Damn Bad Fevah you will get when you go into the jungle-ah, to shoot Tigah.' He guided us in his kindly way through the details of the domestic lives of malaria parasites and of their hosts, the Anopheles mosquitoes, and we learned to recognize under the microscope human blood cells infected with the pretty coloured rings and dots of the parasites. Less than six months later I was seeing them every day and becoming heartily sick of them. We learned also about other tropical illnesses: hookworm, bilharzia, dengue, sandfly fever and scrub typhus, of which I was later to see too much.

My last week at the School of Tropical Medicine was disturbed. Betty knew of course about my embarkation leave and suddenly wrote to suggest that we get married and spend my leave as a honeymoon. As I sat in the lecture rooms of Gower Street my head was filled with delicious pictures of making love to Betty for two weeks on end in some remote cottage. I was 24 years old and my upbringing in a Welsh Calvinistic Methodist community, followed by English public school and university, had left me young for my age. I knew already that I fell in love very easily and that, guided by a deep instinct to be free, I shied away from relationships when they threatened to become lasting; in another age we might have had less of a problem, but this was 1943 and we were prisoners of our generation and class.

Whatever my passing fancies, I was devoted to my mother, and during my last fortnight at home she deserved most of my attention. It was a time of great strain for her. She was a stalwart character who had been widowed when my father was killed in France during the last months of the First World War, before I was born. Photographs taken of her then show her as young and attractive; she was also strong-minded. Assisted by her several brothers and sisters she brought me up and saw to it that I had the best education that she could afford. We were helped out by my getting one or two scholarships and attending school as a day boy, which was cheaper than boarding, but in schoolboy eyes demeaning: day boys were 'skytes' at Shrewsbury. She even bought a house in Shrewsbury and we moved there to live. For her it might as well have been a foreign country, and Shrewsbury still the town where the alien Welsh were put out each night across the Severn over the 'Welsh Bridge'. She must often have been lonely. She and I always had a good relationship except when we talked of religion, for she was deeply religious, and this was a matter on which I rebelled as soon as I began to think for myself. We never let our differences impair our mutual affection and respect, and the love between us remained strong to the end of her life.

At Corwen we were joined for part of my leave by Betty and by an old family friend some 30 years my senior and much attached to me. At this time in my life I was too naive to see in him anything abnormal and for someone to attach himself to me seemed the most wonderful thing in the world. I had shared with him my intense enjoyment of the outdoor world, and he, on his part, had done his best to pass on to me his enjoyment of literature, art and music. He had once been a schoolmaster and indulged the habit of giving advice; much was good and some of that I followed. Our relationship, which continued for many years, gradually fell apart as misunderstandings arose, but the letters I wrote to him during the war provided descriptive material which I have used to fill out the diary entries from which this book was put together.

During my leave the four of us endured days charged with emotion. We took long walks across country in what continued to be a fine autumn. The friend was now launched in full career on advice about the dangers of a precipitate marriage. Betty was of the party but now in a minority of one, though my mother, unlike the friend, made no comment and gave no advice either about marriage or about the future. After a good deal of talk and a bit of thinking I took a decision that was not then or later to make Betty or me happy: we became 'engaged' and that was all.

On 4 November I returned briefly to Crookham to become part of a 'draft' which was to be kitted out and moved on; we had no identities except a corporate one given by the mysterious letters *RCYAG* which we were told to stencil on our baggage. We did not understand the meaning of the code until we reached Bombay together; after that our mail, addressed with those letters, reached us all over India. After a day in which to pack and to be medically inspected we were posted to another depot in Leeds where we were issued with a mountain of kit. The most useful item was a 'bedding roll' made of stout canvas, shaped to hold blankets, sheets, pillow, mosquito net and other belongings. Mine went with me nearly everywhere and I used it long after leaving the army. I was also given an assortment of old-fashioned camping gear which included a clumsy camp bed, canvas bath, canvas wash hand-basin on collapsible wooden frame, canvas bucket and so on; I felt as if we might be going somewhere with Kitchener of Khartoum. The most old-fashioned bit of equipment was a 'Solar Topi', an enormous pith helmet of a design that could not have changed since before the Boer War. Everyone on my draft had a topi, but outside Leeds I never saw one worn; the myth of the need for them had been discarded years before and my last sight of them was at sea near Bombay where they were being thrown over the side of the ship to float in our wake like dead leaves. The last thing given to me, and the least wanted, was a Smith and Wesson revolver, together with a short lecture on how serious it would be for me if I lost it. We had been taught nothing about handling any kind of weapon and even now we were not supplied with any ammunition.

The Commandant of the Depot told us that we should be going to India and that the voyage would take anything up to six weeks. We were given detailed plans for moving twelve MOs and 700 men through the streets of Leeds by night, seeing them into a railway train, and on to a troopship moored in the Clyde. At a final parade near the depot a huge man in the uniform of a Regimental Sergeant Major told me that he had 'never seen such a shower, Sir', indicating 700 undersized men drawn up to be inspected by the ADMS, the senior RAMC officer of the area. The men had a disconsolate look; they were weighed down by packs and kitbags, and wore clothes that seemed several sizes too large. Some wore the Solar Topi that had just been issued. In the drizzle of a Leeds November morning their bodies were dwarfed by such enormous protection against tropical sun and they looked puny and forlorn.

The sights and sounds the night we left Leeds sent shivers down my spine: column of threes, full marching order, kitbags over every shoulder, and the singing in time with the tramp of feet – Roll out the Barrel, Tipperary, Siegfried Line. The drizzle had stopped and a cold north wind was blowing. Broken clouds drove across the full moon, making it look as if the moon itself were hurrying across the dark spaces of the sky. We marched down the cobbled streets, the men out of their billets at last, but knowing nothing of where they were going – not the port, not the continent even. People in hundreds came out of their houses to watch us pass. The local girls got in among the ranks and there was a lot of haphazard kissing. The emotion was too much for one young soldier who had a fit and was left unconscious on the road. Our special train reached Gourock on the following morning and drew up on a quay from which we could dimly see a number of ships anchored out in the Clyde. One of these was our trooper, H.M. Transport *Ranchi*, 16,000 tons, a converted P & O passenger liner. There would be 4000 of us on board. Wrapped in greatcoats against the cold north wind, we waited until it was our turn to climb down into the lighter that was ferrying troops to the ship. Ken Arkle, a young doctor I had met on the way to Leeds, stood with me in the bows, tasting the salt spray as the lighter turned into the waves; we could see mountains to the north and west and I found that he was as interested in them as I was. He was a tall, lanky young man with black hair and his hollow cheeks and twisted smile gave him a satanic look. He had a quiet, biting wit. We got on together at once and were good friends until we reached India and he was posted to Wingate's Chindits.

Chapter 2

H.M. Trooper Ranchi

THE COLD SALT wind, the crying of gulls and the tarry smells of the deck gave place below to the humming of generators and fans and the stale oily scent of warm air. Ken and I shouldered our way down to 'B' deck to find our cabin, which had once been a comfortable cabin for two; the furniture had been stripped to make room for double-decker bunks made of canvas laced to iron frames. We were not far above the waterline and heavy glass in a round brass frame closed our two portholes when at sea. At night close-fitting black covers were clamped over the glass so that no lights showed when we darkened ship. There were eleven of us in the cabin, a mixture of doctors and Royal Engineers. The engineers were already settled in and we were on Christian name terms within minutes. Gomez, our cabin steward, came in night and morning to close or open the portholes and deal with the blackout. He was Goanese, plump, cheerful, olive in complexion and almost bald. He had spent his life at sea with 'The P & O' and wore their steward's uniform, dark trousers and a white coat with brass buttons.

I went on deck to look round; a steady west wind was blowing and the grey shapes of ships at anchor were vague and indistinct in mist and rain. The *Ranchi* was just off the town of Gourock; farther offshore I could make out a cruiser, aircraft carriers, several waiting troopships and in the distance the *Queen Elizabeth*. Lighters went to and fro between the ships and the shore; the big naval ships were motionless, and to come upon them abruptly like this from inland Britain brought a sudden awareness of their power. A destroyer flying the White Ensign swept past us as though we did not exist, and the imperious flashing of signal lamps up and down the river, but never at us, made me feel that we had

11

now come under the care of professionals who spoke all the time but only to each other. We were cargo, and the efficiency and indifference of the Fleet made me feel that our only possible response was grateful subservience.

The decks were crowded; as well as engineers and RAMC, we had nursing sisters on board, airmen, gunners, men from the Ordnance Corps and Marine Commandos. I went below to see our men's quarters and was dismayed to find how crowded they were. In the mess decks they were eating and living at long wooden tables; at night they slung their hammocks head to tail from beams above the tables, so close as often to be touching. It was hot down there and ventilation was poor; men already in their hammocks were naked to the waist. I wondered what sort of hell this would be when we were at sea and they were seasick, or later, in the heat of the tropics. And what if a torpedo or a bomb arrived here in the bowels of the boat!

In the evening of 14 November, after dark, above the ordinary noises of the ship, we heard the throb of engines and the *Ranchi* began quietly to slip down the Clyde. Ken and I stood on the tarpaulin-covered forward hatch; by moonlight I could pick out the outlines of Arran and Bute, places where I had gone sailing while still at school. Arran grew larger and clearer and we slowed down to drop the Pilot. There was snow on the island and cloud hid the tops of the hills; the sea was calm and the only wind was that made by our own movement. Ken and I talked about the stars and I recalled once being shown the distant nebula in Andromeda, so distant as to be outside our galaxy; we picked it out and with the help of other stars judged that we were steaming slightly west of south. When I woke next morning I saw land to port and on the starboard quarter; we were coming out of the North Channel and were in the middle of a big convoy. Soon we began to pitch in the Atlantic swell. For the next ten days we made a big circle westwards before heading for the Mediterranean, and during that time the ship was full of rumour and guesswork about where we were going. We tried to track our position day by day from our zig-zag course. The airmen on board made a crude sextant with stiff cardboard and by roughly calculating the sun's declination were able to make very good guesses at our latitude.

One day might differ from another in detail, but the life of the ship followed an unchanging pattern set by the demands of safety at sea in wartime and the routine of eating, sleeping, washing and taking exercise. There were regular calls to 'Boat Stations' after breakfast and occasional surprise calls during the day to keep us on our toes. My station for the boats was No. 14, near a long-barrelled 6 in. gun mounted on the after deck. We were on the deck below the boat deck, and the boats would be swung out and down to our level for us to step into them. At Station 14 there were two lifeboats and 230 men. Each lifeboat held fifty men but there were also Carley floats lashed on the upper decks; if the *Ranchi* was badly hit and sank, those who survived the chaos below and could not find room in a boat might be able to climb on one of the floats. In case of abandoning ship we each had a kapok life jacket which we carried all day wherever we went.

Like all troopships the *Ranchi* was a 'dry' ship, but, however unsatisfactory the arrangements for drinking might be, no one could complain about the food. When she had last come from America her cold stores had been filled with meat, fruit and vegetables, and we, coming from rationed England, were fed in a way that we had forgotten.

The army officers permanently aboard in charge of troops did not make a good impression on us. We were frustrated and angry about the lack of interest in the men's ailments shown by the army doctors who belonged to the ship and by their refusal to put at our disposal as doctors the means of treating even the simplest illnesses. It was galling when we knew that there were among us good doctors with half a lifetime of experience. As unattached MOs we kept an eye ourselves on the 700 RAMC other ranks; we visited their quarters, inspected their food, listened to complaints, gave out pay and censored letters. We were all depressed at reading over and over again the same messages in every sort of misspelt and illiterate form. Never in these letters did I come across anything censorable, any breach of security, and to read them might have seemed an intrusion into other men's privacy if their contents had not mirrored our own feelings. After two days so spent we thought of the *Ranchi* as a boatload of love-lorn transportees.

Steaming east in a flat calm one day I saw a submarine on the surface and beyond it the faint outline of the African coast; at dusk what looked like a lighthouse appeared to the north, and the ship put out what we called 'Spoon baits'; the proper name for them was 'Paravanes'. They were a bit like the otter boards used by trawlers and were streamed to port and starboard from the bow on long steel hawsers; they were meant to catch and move away from the ship any mines that might lie in our path now that we were in shallow waters. Another change was that from a winch on deck we flew a barrage balloon on the end of a long cable; we were within range of enemy air attack. The ships of the convoy steamed in line ahead in single file.

After Boat Stations on 25 November we had an hour's lecture on speaking Urdu, lingua franca of the army in India; then, after an hour's P.T., we sat round waiting for lunch. Ken was reading *The Idiot* and I was halfway through *Paradise Lost*. Satan, the great voyager in the wild and waste parts of the earth, had become my hero. We knew that we were in the Mediterranean and during the afternoon we passed a hilly point projecting from the African shore somewhere east of Oran.

At 0800 next morning we passed a fairly large town; its squarer white buildings faced north-east and were backed by hills. I guessed it to be Algiers. Two ships left the convoy and headed shorewards. After tea that afternoon the strident ringing of alarm bells sounded for Action Stations as the convoy was attacked by Heinkels and torpedo bombers. One ship was hit and set on fire, a column of black smoke rising into the still air long after the raid was over. We were told that four Heinkels ended up in the sea and that several Spitfires were lost. My post in an attack was a First Aid Post on C Deck, at the foot of the main staircase, rather forward of the bridge and not much above the waterline. Alleys crowded with men led to the mess decks. The sound of gunfire from above was deafening, a continuous rapid clattering of Oerlikon guns and the slower 'boom boom boom' of the heavier calibre Bofors with which the ship was also armed. A gunner came to me with a smashed finger and I put on a dressing before sending him to the ship's MO. The next morning the BBC's version of last night's raid came over the ship's radio: 'Allied convoy attacked in Mediterranean with loss of eight enemy and a few allied planes; negligible damage to the convoy'. It was my first experience of the broadcasting of an event at which I had been present and it led to a distrust of reporters which lasted all my life.

Action Stations sounded again at 1645 on 29 November, and I rushed down to my post on C deck. The men hated the mess decks when they could hear gunfire and knew that bombs were dropping. They crowded round me and I had great difficulty in keeping the alleyways clear. They sat on the floor, stood around, talked, smoked and all the time asked for news from on deck. Above the sound of the guns we could hear the explosions of distant bombs. Suddenly there was a tremendous crash overhead, followed by a deafening explosion and the sound of running water forward. Tension mounted and there was a rush towards me along the alleyways. I thought, 'This must be what panic is' and did not at all feel like trying to push past to see if anyone farther forward was hurt. All at once they were quiet again as the noise from above died down. The attack was over. A 500 lb delayed action bomb set to go off when well down in the ship had been heading for the *Ranchi's* bridge when it was deflected by a steel stay, smashed through the deck forward of our position and left the ship by way of the side plating, not exploding until near the water. I heard that one man afterwards sat unable to move, staring at the hole it made in the deck as it passed him; three men were injured by flying rivets, one of them fatally.

Next day we passed Tobruk at lunchtime and Bardia in the evening, names well known to us from news about the war in the Western Desert, but places oddly unreal to us now that we were close at hand. We left the convoy the following morning and the other twelve ships steamed on; land came into sight to starboard, a mirage at first. At Boat Stations that day the look of the sea was always changing, more beautiful than ever; there were great stretches of light blue-green, and darker patches of deep reddish blue and violet where the surface was ruffled by wind squalls. The sun was bright and there were few clouds as we entered Alexandria Harbour.

The *Ranchi* was barely anchored when she was surrounded by 'bumboats' manned by Egyptians wearing red fez and dirty white 'nighties'. In some there were negroes with skins of a marvellous glossy black. They manoeuvred alongside and threw lines to us. Small naked boys dived for the coins we threw into the muddy water, and before our eyes stretched the seafront of Alexandria, splendid, brilliantly white, a crescent of tall buildings, domes and minarets. On deck a busy, laughing crowd of soldiers leant over the rail arguing the price of oranges and melons and pulling up baskets of fruit and a succession of leather goods: handbags, suit-cases, decorated 'poufs'. They would not have been so merry if they had known that we were to be there at anchor for eleven days. No one was allowed ashore and, except for port officials, no one came aboard. For days there was no news, only rumour. Trained as I was for a demanding profession, but with no work and no responsibilities, and seeming to be no nearer the war, those eleven days on the *Ranchi*, followed by three weeks in a transit camp, were the most miserable of my life.

On 12 December, 1943, we disembarked and moved to Camp 190 at Sidi Bishr, six miles east of Alexandria, past King Fouad's private harbour in which the water was a clear and lovely blue. Ken and I shared a tent which was roomy enough for us to spread our luggage and camp furniture. Date palms gave shade, and the sea shore was less than 100 yards away; farther out, but within swim-ming distance, rollers broke gently on a long reef. The officers' mess was in a large tent where every kind of drink was to be had; we were served by Palestinians and Italian POWs. As MOs our days were passed doing small jobs like sick parades and repeated health inspections. We read, waited for meals and attended parades for PT, for Church (C of E here, RC over there), for route marches and for swimming. I enjoyed taking the men to the beach by the camp; the water was warm, a clear greeny blue, and the sea was never rough.

Ken and I decided to get out of camp as much as possible and one day, after a route march and a swim with the men, the two of us took a tram into Alexandria as far as the Summer Palace. The tram conductor blew a shrill and plaintive note on a little trumpet to signal to the driver when he wanted to start or stop. After lunch at a restaurant we went to the harbour, and at the water's edge came on an old boatbuilder. Flat on the sand at his feet was a wooden board several feet square made of planks fastened edge to edge; on it had been marked with a sharp tool the shape of every frame of the boat that he was going to build, in effect an architect's drawing of the sections of a boat; it was a typical small Arab felucca. For how many centuries, we wondered, had these simple shapes been handed down like this on templates of wood. Using the marks as guides, the old man cut the frames out of wide planks with a gigantic fretsaw and set them up on the keel before the final planking. We saw one of his finished boats, a beamy craft with attractive lines. He showed us how he smoothed off the curves of the hull with a very sharp adze. He and the two small boys who helped him were as pleased as they were surprised to find two strangers in Army uniform interested in their work.

Every few days one or other of us went down with 'Gippy tummy', diarrhoea and vomiting. In addition I had a fever that was classified as FEVER, N.Y.D. – 'not yet diagnosed'. My friends, glad of a diversion from the deadly monotony, hovered over me, pooled their knowledge and decided I must have sand-fly or 'break-bone' fever. When Boyd, a middle-aged ex-GP, told the gathering that I was on no account to get up, I lay back with relief: I had a headache and my bones really were hurting. All day I could hear the high-pitched wailing voice of our laundry boy as he ran about the camp collecting and delivering washing and plaintively calling out, "Flyin' dhobie – washin'," then breaking off into a weird and mournful song in his own language. Egypt was my first sight of what was later called 'The Third World' and it made me sad.

I saw more of it when I was detailed with another MO to inoculate 1200 coolies against typhus at a Base Supply Depot on the other side of Alexandria. They waited for us, frightened, in a huge compound, squatting in the shade, grinning nervously and gesticulating. Ragged and dirty, pockmarked and covered with scabs and boils, they were herded like beasts, and driven towards us in groups of twenty by men armed with long whips which they used freely. Our routine was to gesture 'Roll up your sleeve', put on a dab of spirit and say a few Arabic words we had been taught – 'Not to worry' 'Good chap' 'Finished now', and a useful word 'Yallah' that seemed to mean 'Off you go'. After the jab they worked the inoculated arm violently up and down and gave a sort of grimacing smile, dreadful to see. We were told that the coolies were well paid – 20 piastres (about two shillings) a day.

I wanted to see the Pyramids and Ken said that he would come with me. We did not ask for leave because we did not think it would be granted; but to see Cairo would be worth any minor scrape in which we might land ourselves. The train journey from Alexandria took us first over flat, fertile irrigated country; later high ground appeared in the distance, sandy-coloured or bluish from far off, its escarpments brought into sharp relief by sun and shadow; the high lands lay east and west, divided by the deep green of the Nile valley. We went through banana plantations and Government farms; trees were plentiful: orange groves, poplars, palms, willows, and cactus caked with sand or mud. Over the tree-tops we could see the lateen sails of boats gliding slowly along the canals of the delta. We passed towns and villages, small compact groups of buildings made of mud or brick; on the flat roofs were heaps of dung being dried for fuel. Here and there were domes and towers and in one village a dovecote.

People squatted idly on the banks of waterways or worked in a leisurely way in the fields. We passed donkeys hurrying along earth tracks and strings of camels with their halting, stately gait. Veiled women in black rode with bent heads on the backs of donkeys while their men walked barefoot, carrying shoes in their hands, only putting them on their feet when riding. We saw the Nile fishermen carrying fine white nets hung from poles. Many of the birds we had not seen before; there were kites, kestrels and other small hawks, kingfishers, egrets, hooded crows, lapwings, woodpeckers and flocks of brilliant black and white birds, in flight very like sandpipers. We noticed everything because all was new to us; we were free and laughed delightedly, like two children let out of school.

We saw different ways of drawing water for irrigation; it could be dipped out of a canal from the Nile with a bucket hung on the end of a balanced pole; it could be wound out with a long wooden Archimedes screw operated by hand, the like of which I had never expected to see outside a textbook of elementary physics; or it could be drawn from wells by oxen: the ox walked round the parapet of a well and turned a long beam geared to a spindle that wound the water bucket from the depths on the end of a rope.

Cairo from a distance was less fine than Alexandria but the streets were spacious and had a more western look; the shops, restaurants and hotels looked modern and more prosperous than those of Alexandria. Betty's brother Robert worked there at GHQ Middle East and was, I think, 'something in intelligence' to do with Greece. He entertained us to lunch in the luxurious surroundings of his top-floor flat, introducing us to sweet lemons which I have not tasted anywhere else. Robert and I must have surreptitiously examined each other: I did not at once take to him, being unable on such short acquaintance to make up my mind. He was quicker and more shrewd, for he wrote to his sister to say that I seemed to be someone who did not know where he was going. How right he was! Being stuck in Egypt with no plan for the future and nothing useful to do made me rudderless. I was unsure of myself and had begun already to doubt my readiness to commit myself to something as serious as marriage. When we said that we should like to see the Pyramids while we were there, a request rather like an American in London saying that he wants to 'Do the Tower', Robert advised us to take a taxi to Gizeh. Once we had escaped from the crowd of dragomen that surrounded us there we found we could stroll around almost unmolested. The middle pyramid (that of Khefren) retained on the upper part its ancient facing of alabaster and we decided that one day we must return to climb it. We spent most of the afternoon gazing at the Sphinx, the chubby cheeks, famous smile and slightly broken nose.

On 9 January we were told that we should be moving on. I was baggage officer again, on the principle that if you've once done a job you'll get it next time a name is wanted for it. First came the order 'Men will take kitbags on the train with them'. Then 'All kitbags will go in a luggage van at the rear of the train'. The empty train arrived and I could see that its rear was where I expected to see its front. By the time I had mobilized baggage parties and begun to move kitbags our very agitated colonel had arrived, preoccupied only with getting a compartment to himself. At Sidi Gabir outside Alexandria the train picked up some Nursing Sisters who also had their minds on their specially reserved places.

We waited for an hour at the next stop and when I strolled on the platform I noticed that the engine boiler was heated by an oil and water splash fire, the only one I had seen except at the Army School of Hygiene. A barefoot urchin came up to me and said, 'Where you go?' Security minded, I replied, 'Who knows?' He grinned and said with assurance, 'You go Port Tewfik.' I ought to have known; this was the East and our destination was probably known in all the bazaars from Tunis to Bombay, and not of much interest to anyone either.

At Ben Ha the train left the Cairo line and turned east into the desert. Some time after dawn we reached Port Tewfik, a barren place on the Sinai shore of the Gulf of Suez, where a ship was moored to a quay. She was the *City of London*, black and small, less than half the size of the *Ranchi*, but unlike the *Ranchi* she looked like a ship rather than a block of flats. We filed aboard and from the deck looked down at coolies waiting on the quay to bring baggage off the train. Like those I had inoculated at Alexandria, they were herded into groups and over each group stood a man with a long lash. The custom was that when a ship was alongside, these unfortunates were brought on the quay and waited crouching until there was a job to do. As the British engineer sergeant in charge of loading said, 'They've no minds of their own, Sir. You can do what you like with them.' It was horrible.

The *City of London* had not been completely gutted for trooping and our cabins were snug, with proper bunks and fans. Ken and I shared a cabin with Robert Boyd; he was short, plump and almost hairless, and slept a great deal; I sometimes wondered if he suffered from a deficiency of the thyroid gland; he had that look, but I never asked him. He was always quietly kind and was a very good doctor.

We were lucky in the Red Sea to have a fresh southerly wind which countered the heat which is felt in those waters when the wind is astern. The sea was a deep bright blue dotted with small breaking crests. Except for some rocky islands we saw no land until we reached Aden, where we anchored out in the bay. In the background was a line of jagged hills. It was cloudless and hot; fragile-looking boats came alongside to trade, and kites, vultures and gulls circled overhead. By the afternoon many of the kites had settled in various attitudes on our foremast. Water was scarce at Aden: it might rain perhaps once a year, and the longest recorded drought in recent times had lasted five years.

I watched over the ship's side one of the light native boats that came out to us – 'buoyant as a fulmar on the waves'. It was pointed at the ends, high-prowed and altogether beautiful on the transparent blue-green sea. It was rigged with one mast and a single lateen sail, and manned by two near naked giants with close curly hair and skins the colour of dark-roasted coffee beans. A big swell ran past our anchored ship; the light bubbling foam on the wave crests and the deeper streaks of green farther out remain in the memory. The effortless way the light boat moved and the easy skill of its laughing crew were intoxicating: "Buy wine of us, you English brig."

After we left Aden I went down with diarrhoea and colicky pains, and Boyd, who was himself quite as ill, put me on 'Sulfa' drugs and a diet of nothing but iced lime juice. Next day I gave myself a grain of opium to settle my stomach and went back to bed. I had a series of wild and improbable dreams which lasted until late afternoon when I rushed on deck, hearing cries of 'Torpedo, torpedo'. Everyone was crowded along the starboard rail gazing at the approaching torpedo when it suddenly altered course near the ship and changed into a school of dolphin; they formed up in line ahead before our bows, a beautiful, splashing joyous company.

I made friends with some Merchant Navy officers in the cabin next to ours; they answered my endless questions about how to navigate a ship by the sun and stars, lent me books and taught me enough for me to write a useful account for some future day. Like us, they were only on passage in the *City of London*, but they took me to the bridge and gave me practical lessons on the use of the sextant. Aden was the most southerly point on our route to Bombay and on the night we left I got a sentry to wake me at 0400 to see the Southern Cross. It was easy to find, but so many glorious stars and constellations shone in that southern sky that I was disappointed. The Pole Star was low on the horizon and the Milky Way made a smaller crescent than I was used to.

I enjoyed going to the very stem of the ship on fine nights. The strong warm headwind whistled round my ears and the sea raced past, the bow-wave turning over in white breakers and a great glow of phosphorescence. "Blows the cobwebs away, doesn't it," said a young soldier who had joined me. For me it blew away a lot more besides: it blew away doubts and sadnesses; I knew now that I must do my job where I was going and put off thinking about any future until I got home. Ahead the black water rushed smoothly towards the ship, reflecting the light of a million stars from its not yet broken surface: Kipling's 'planet-powdered floors'.

Large schools of dolphin followed by clouds of sea birds were with us every day after we left Aden; the lascars said, "Fish convoy with aeroplanes, Sahib." We saw flying fish all day; their bodies from above looked black and their fins transparent; they left the water in little groups of about half a dozen, fanning out to left and right in mid-air and gliding near the surface, very fast, for forty yards or more, only occasionally touching the crest of a wave.

Three days before we reached Bombay the ship's MO (Troops) gave us a lecture about life in India; I went back to our cabin afterwards and found Ken sitting gloomily on his bunk eating bread and bully beef as fast as he could. Various friends drifted in and it seemed that the MO had cast deep gloom over all of us, chiefly by saying that we were going to be four or five years in the Far East.One newly married doctor was very depressed; he sat with his face in his hands listening to us rehearsing the disappointments and miseries conjured up by the ill-timed talk. At last he looked up and said, "I don't want to *know* anything about India. I just – don't – want – to – know about it."

We came into Bombay soon after noon on 22 January, 1944. Small hilly islands began to show, and clumps of trees; there were porpoises in the muddy water alongside and dozens of kites appeared; the men threw scraps for the kites to catch in mid-air and yelled in chorus at each daring swoop and clever catch. We passed the 'Gateway to India' without noticing and berthed at the Mackenzie Pier, Bombay, before tea. We set about filling in forms and changing money.

The climax of the voyage for all of us was at last to find mail from home. For two and a half months we had been cut off from all that home meant to us and if there was anyone who had no letters that day he must have been very lonely. I settled in a corner to go through my letters slowly, one by one, and wherever I looked men were doing the same, standing motionless or sitting on the deck, going through letter after letter.

Our draft was split up at Bombay and we were posted as 'general duty officers' to British Military Hospitals all over India. Ken and I were posted together; we were to go to Cawnpore, nearly a thousand miles from Bombay – two days and a night by train. Boyd came with us as far as Jhansi where, presumably because he had a Diploma in Public Health, he was posted as a specialist in epidemics, drinking water and drains. Except for chance encounters with Gunn and Dawson, I saw no more of the others.

Chapter 3

India

ON THE MORNING after reaching Bombay Ken and I were taken by truck with five other doctors and several nurses to Victoria Terminus, Bombay's main railway station, and I was suddenly plunged into India. My first impressions were of noise and squalor and restless movement, of human tragedy begging for relief that I could not give and from which I felt coldly insulated. My tin trunk was hoisted on the turbaned head of a coolie wearing a dirty red cotton tunic and the next minute saw my bedding roll lifted as well and balanced on top of the tin trunk. The man turned and on spindly legs moved off with bent knees towards our train. Coolies jogged with huge loads in every direction; sellers of sweetmeats called out, "*Misri, jelebi, jelebi*" and displayed the sticky sugary confections on basketware trays. There was a cry of "*Chae, garm chae*", "Tea, hot tea" from men with urns or aluminium kettles and stacks of small brown earthenware cups; after drinking from a cup you dashed it to the ground. Adding to the general clamour of beggars was the high-pitched call of the cigarette-sellers, "*Pan, biri*, cigarette"; *pan* advertised the leaf, betelnut and lime paste for chewing betel, and *biri* the small rolled green leaf with an acrid smoke used by those unable to afford cigarettes.

We had been given our train tickets when we left the ship and someone had reserved places for us in two–berth first-class accommodation. When our luggage had been stowed we climbed up and found a compartment the width of the train with two leather-covered bunks, one above the other, where our bedding had already been unrolled. There was nothing cramped about the compartment and two leather-upholstered fixed chairs for daytime use were part of the furniture. When we turned to stand in the doorway the coolies had been pushed aside by a crowd of beggars: "Baksheesh, Sahib, Bara Sahib. No mother, no father, no brother, no sister; baksheesh Sahib." It went on and on, and every kind of mutilation and deformity was offered for our inspection: stumps of arms and legs, blind eyes, festering sores covered with flies, and we could only marvel at the speed with which some of these terrible cripples could cover the ground from one possible source of alms to another.

The train did not start at once and presently over the heads of the crowd we saw an officer's peaked cap worn at a jaunty angle: it was Maurice, liveliest of our engineer friends on the *Ranchi*. He had been posted to 'Transportation' and was on his way to Deolali, through which we should pass that evening. There was none of the blowing of whistles and slamming of doors to which we were accustomed at home. The Calcutta Mail began its journey silently, smoothly, with less fuss even than the Rome Express leaving the Gare de Lyon, although it had twice as far to go. The chae-wallahs, the coolies still arguing about payment, the bent heads of sari-clad women and the vendors of cigarettes began to slide past our open door; the upstretched pleading arms and clutching hands fell away and became indistinct in the mass of humanity. We gathered speed as we passed by the shanty-town slums of Bombay and the great marshalling yards of Kalyan and began to climb steeply and continuously about strange bare hills where rocky outcrops and fantastic pinnacles showed through the haze. We passed through tunnels and over viaducts. The air at first was hot and the ground in that dry season looked barren and scrubby. Ken remarked on how suited to a colourless landscape were the brightly coloured clothes of the villagers.

We climbed 2000 feet through the Ghats to the plateau of the Great Indian Plain before stopping to change engines from electric to steam. As evening came on we saw habitation and animals: groups of thatched huts with mud walls, bullocks with birds perched on their backs. In the background dimly seen ranges of hills encircled us and rock spires towered into the sky; it was not at all what we had expected to see in India. The sun set deep red below streaky clouds; twilight lasted but half an hour and the stars came out with a rush.

Maurice left us at Deolali where we ordered dinner to be served at a station farther along the line. When the train waited at such halts flocks of green parakeets screamed like swifts overhead as they flew at high speed to the trees, where they squawked restlessly before roosting. We ate dinner in our compartment and I then settled on my bunk, wrapped in a blanket, for it was suddenly chilly after nightfall, to read my letters. Under their influence I was soon back home walking the country lanes with Betty when Ken, who had had fewer letters than I, began to complain that I had gone into a trance, stretched out on the bunk "like a bloody pasha", subconsciously reaching out a hand now and then for a banana from the bunch on the table. Next day we telegraphed ahead from wayside stations to arrange for meals and at pre-arranged halts were served with *chota hazri* or early morning tea and toast, and later with breakfast, lunch and tea. Robert Boyd stayed in our compartment for much of the second day but left us at Jhansi which we reached early in the afternoon. We sat all day in the doorway or by the open window on the shaded side of the train, gazing at the passing country and seeing on telegraph wires and in the open a countless variety of colourful birds completely new to us: vultures, kites, drongos, bee-eaters, shrikes of several kinds, rollers. I began to think that I might find a lot in India to interest me.

Soon after Jhansi we crossed the Jumna which rises far to the north in the snows beyond Dehra Dun and flows past Delhi and Agra to join the Ganges below Cawnpore. In the dry season the river was not very wide and only the great extent of the girders which spanned the sandy banks on either side showed how big it must be in the rains. Towards evening on the second day we saw with regret that we were slowing down on the outskirts of a large, drab industrial town. At the side of the track ungainly vultures as big as turkeys were busy feeding, plunging bloody heads and necks deep in the carcase of a dead cow. We had reached Cawnpore. Before the train stopped we were beset by red-smocked coolies who hung on the doors eager to take our luggage. I stood at the station entrance surrounded by baggage, refusing the offers of Sikh drivers with large taxis to take us wherever we liked, while Ken telephoned the British Military Hospital to say that we had arrived. I had been advised about the payment of coolies (four annas 'per package per trip') but when I had paid out the miserable sums the coolies looked at me and at the small coins in their palms and cried. "What is this, Sahib? What is this? I am poor man, Sahib." If there were no outcry, I thought, hardening my heart, it would mean that I had given too much. An Army truck arrived from the hospital and, brushing aside the importunate Sikhs, we had our baggage lifted in and climbed up ourselves by the driver.

At the hospital we were directed to a bungalow in more open country not far from the Ganges. Two RAMC captains, Guggenheim and Heathcote, greeted us and showed us a bedroom we could share. They lent us their bearer or personal servant to make up beds and wait on us at table until we engaged our own servants. The bungalow was spacious; the verandahs were wide and cool and the house stood in open parkland where the trees were always in leaf and gave shade. On our first morning after a leisurely breakfast we walked to the hospital and were shown over the British wing. A doctor and a sister took us round the almost empty wards and introduced us to the few in-patients, sufferers either from melancholia or from obscure fevers which no one had been able to diagnose. A small isolation ward stood apart and we were taken there to be shown two soldiers with very bad smallpox, rather as we might be taken by the curator of Kew Gardens to see prized shrubs of which he was particularly proud. One of these patients was English and the other a West African negro; we had not seen advanced smallpox before and I never forgot the sight of their purulent sores and extreme illness.

We spent what was left of the morning finding our way about the cantonment and visiting the Post Office, the Club and the Station Office. We discovered that in India the simplest kind of shopping demanded the help of a servant. An official at the Post Office explained in English that the only way to remain calm and dignified and yet get things done was by not doing them yourself. Take, for example, sending a cable: to find out what sort of cable was appropriate for your needs (itself no simple matter in India) and to obtain a form on which to write your message, you did not attend the Post Office in person; you did not join a queue, enter the hurlyburly of an Indian crowd or go near a counter. Your bearer did these things. When you had written the cable you handed it to him to take back to the Post Office for transmission. These things were what a bearer was for. He did them for you while you lay back in a cane chair at the club with a long cool drink. We were not received with much enthusiasm at the Cawnpore Club. We went there for drinks before lunch on a Sunday and stood feeling very much the outsiders, surrounded by a buzz of coded 'station' talk so private that we wondered, not for the last time, if any of these people had any idea why we were in India, or that the India in which they lived was fighting a war. Militarily, Cawnpore was an 'Area' commanded by a Brigadier, and I was soon given to understand that I was expected to observe certain customs: for example, officers were not to be seen carrying parcels. This, like a host of small things in British India, irritated me. It meant that if I bought a few books in town, I was expected to hire an urchin to carry them wherever I went on foot.

For a bungalow such as ours there was a recognized complement of servants; the least that would do for four of us would be two bearers, a waiter, a cook, a water-carrier and a sweeper, or man of the lowest caste who attended to menial work that no one else would touch. Most of the servants were already in post and Ken and I needed only to find a bearer. We casually mentioned in the hearing of the servants that a second bearer was needed and presently an assortment of men stood before us. Each carried in his hand a collection of 'chitties', much-thumbed scraps of paper scribbled over with references, some of them enigmatic, from previous employers. We chose an old white-haired man of about 60, whose lined brown face, drooping white moustache and fine forehead appealed to us. He was called Jafar Ali and for 50 rupees a month agreed to act as bearer for Ken and me.

Jafar Ali immediately set about ordering our lives, arranging through a local contractor (who had some undisclosed link with the station office) to hire bicycles and furniture for us. He did my everyday shopping, posted letters and sent cables, always charging a small commission on whatever he did, and being scrupulously careful always to explain to me, when presenting the bill, the presence and amount of this item. I liked him.

My afternoons were usually free and I often went into town on a bicycle. The days were only moderately hot and I cycled slowly through the bazaars doing my best to avoid pedestrians and the holy cows which lay half asleep in the roadways and on the pavements. I enjoyed watching craftsmen at work in their open-fronted shops as I took in the sounds and smells and sniffed at exotic scents whose origins I did not know. The pavements were splashed with purplish-red betel spit. Indian policemen stood at cross-roads, neatly turned out in shorts, leather belts, puttees and boots, with smart puggarees on their heads. They carried batons with which they went through the motions of directing traffic after it had passed, half-heartedly waving to cars already distant, approving the event with appropriate signals.

We wore khaki drill: shorts and knee-length 'stocking tops' which allowed us to change our sweaty socks often, without needing a big supply of full-length stockings. When not formally dressed we wore heavy sandals known as 'chaplis'. In the bazaar I looked at several pairs and, unable to make up my mind which of two pairs would suit me, asked, "Which is the better pair?" There was a non-committal shrug of the shoulders and that slight sideways movement of the head, indescribable and unmistakeable, which means both assent and, "Just as you please, Sahib. Both are better, Sahib."

I was left to muse, as I cycled home, whether 'better' in this country of ambiguities might also mean 'excellent'. I had already discovered that in the Urdu language *kal*, which meant tomorrow, also meant yesterday, and *parson*, which was the day after tomorrow, was also the day before yesterday. The bazaars were full of the scent of spices and I liked the warmth of the air and the greenery of the great shady trees at the side of the road. As I cycled back I saw monkeys sitting by the road in human attitudes: dejected, chin on hand, or half asleep in the heat of the afternoon, head back and hands folded over belly. On the soft earth that flanked the roads coolies carrying huge loads on their heads went with a peculiar kind of jogging gait, a lurching run, and with them bullock carts drawn by sad-looking downtrodden water buffaloes.

Ken was suddenly posted for training in the jungle with a special force; after a few days he came back and told us that he would be moving away for good. Months later I had a letter from him telling me that he was somewhere in Burma with a 'Long Range Penetration Group'. After he had gone my days at Cawnpore began to drag.

I now saw more of Guggenheim, a large, genial man who had been in general practice in London before the war. He was a refugee from Nazi Germany and insisted, like Ludwig Guttman, that there was something inherently wrong with the German people. We argued about the world after the war; he favoured an international police force for the future and painted a glowing picture of his ideal, a powerful standing army that would be independent of any one nation. I thought it would never work.

One morning we set off early to walk to the Ganges, which was not far from the bungalow. Even in the dry season the river was vast, brown, relentlessly flowing. Terns and pied kingfishers hovered over it, small turtles showed their heads and backs in it, and were quick to dive out of sight when they saw us. Guggenheim and a friend who had joined us had brought guns with a view to shooting wild geese and while the two of them hired a boat and were paddled to a sandbank I took a stroll along the riverside. Upstream the river stretched to where I could see faintly the outlines of a railway bridge at least a mile long. I was standing where the river turns towards the southeast; the banks were well above the water, perhaps 15 feet high, except at one place where a rough track led down to the water's edge. Not much imagination was needed to conclude that I was not far from the place where in 1857 the survivors of a siege in the open at Cawnpore had embarked with the assurance of a safe conduct; they had been mown down by fire from the river bank directly they climbed into the boats. The women and children who survived were imprisoned by the Nana Sahib and later cut to pieces by the worst of his men; the bodies were thrown into a well which afterwards became part of a memorial garden. I found the well on one of my cycle outings: to be at the scene of those terrible events made them come to life as no history lesson had done, and before I left Cawnpore I questioned Jafar Ali about the Mutiny. His father, he said, had been one of General Havelock's bearers and he himself had heard an account by an eyewitness of the shooting down of the three boatloads of fugitives on the river and of the casting of the bodies into the well. Jafar Ali was 59 years old and his claims were not impossible.

On 8 February I was called to the Commandant's office and told that I was posted to No. 7 Indian Malaria Forward Treatment Unit (7 IMFTU) which was being raised at Lucknow, fifty miles away. I left Cawnpore the next day without regret. When I first reached India I felt, as many others did, instant sympathy with

Indians and some disgust at the overbearing attitude of my own countrymen; the feeling of sympathy gradually gave way to irritation with things Indian and admiration for all that the British had accomplished during their time there. As my train crossed the long bridge over the Ganges I wondered what on earth an IMFTU was.

The IMFTUs

In the dark jungles of the mountain frontier between India and Burma during 1943 and 1944 about one man in five was away from his unit at any one time because of sickness; a company commander who nominally could expect to call on more than 200 men would find in those conditions that forty might not be there. When the casualty returns of XIVth Army for those years were studied it was found that nine out of every ten casualties were due not to Japanese bullets but to sickness, the chief sickness being malaria. There were others of course, like typhus and dysentery, but none ravaged the troops and reduced their numbers as malaria did. One reason for the absenteeism caused by malaria was the slowness of travel; although it might not take more than three weeks to treat a man, it could take months to return him to his unit. An infantryman sent back to a Field Ambulance with malaria might at first be as unfit for duty as if he had a gunshot wound, but he would make a quick recovery. Unfortunately by that time he would often have been evacuated to the rear to clear the Field Ambulance for other casualties; he would have been taken back over congested mountain tracks to a Casualty Clearing Station, and might perhaps have gone even farther by rail to a General Hospital. Although completely recovered and fit to rejoin his platoon, he could by now be 200 miles from his unit, separated first by a single-track narrow-gauge railway running through thick jungle, then a precipitous mountain road whose very existence was a miracle on those steep hillsides covered with rain forest. These were the supply lines of an army and space for forward travel was at a premium.

So the MFTU, or 'Malaria Forward Treatment Unit', was born. It could be set up near the front, at Divisional or even Brigade level like a Field Ambulance; and it could treat patients and return them to their units in quick time. The patients lay on rows of stretchers in tents

31

accommodating about fifty men and were treated with Quinine, Mepacrine and Pamaquin for two to three weeks, after which they went to another camp to get fit. The MFTUs were called 'Indian' because they were 'Indian Army' units and had a mixed staff, more Indian than British, for we treated all troops of XIVth Army. Our IMFTU was No. 7; No. 5, of which I was to see a good deal later, was also being raised at Lucknow, somewhere near us.

No. 7 IMFTU was at Kitchener Lines, on the outskirts of Lucknow. The camp was by a derelict wooded garden beyond La Martinière School, the original of 'St Xavier's' in Kipling's *Kim*. Here we shared 180-pounder tents, about eight foot square; the earth beneath them was dug down to a depth of 18 ins to give head-room, and the tent poles stood on upturned oil drums; the extra height made the tents cool and enabled us to hang mosquito nets over our camp beds. 'The Mess' where we ate was a shelter with a tiled roof but no walls, home for uncounted mosquitoes and flies, and for the small grey lizards that scampered upside down all over the ceiling; the Mess 'Ante-room' was a marquee tent about 20 foot square furnished with a carpet, easy chairs, low tables, a few rugs and a gramophone; a cupboard and trestle table served as a bar.

On my arrival I was greeted by Captain Donaldson (Don) who introduced me to the CO. Lieutenant-Colonel Wakeford was a tall, fairhaired Rhodesian with the build and carriage of an athlete; he wore the ribbon of the North Africa campaign with a 'mention'. He introduced me to the others: a Canadian with whom I was to share a tent, Wallace Parke, the 'Medical Specialist', several Indian doctors, including a Sikh, a South Indian called Kurup, a Bengali and a Punjabi, and Terry, a sallow young man in the Indian Army Medical Corps, whom at first I took to be Welsh because of his sing-song Anglo–Indian voice. I asked him what part of Wales he came from, an unhappy mistake because he was very sensitive about his Eurasian blood. There were also two ex-regular soldiers who had risen from the ranks and had administrative jobs: McKeown, the quartermaster, known as Mac, very Irish and hot-tempered, and Bill Gleed, who had been a sergeant major in the Gloucester Regiment and was called Registrar, a post in some ways like that of adjutant. Altogether they were a friendly lot and I felt at home. John Wakeford was a reserved man and kept himself a little apart, but I knew at once that he was greatly liked and respected. It was a happy Mess and for the first time in the army I had a sense of belonging, of being one of a unit that was going somewhere with a purpose.

The mosquitoes were bad and I was careful to tuck in my net when I went to bed. I did not hear my companion, the Canadian, come into the tent, but he was there in the morning. A servant brought early tea and when I lifted the corner of my net to reach for the mug I could see that the net on the other bed was twitching. After a while a hand came out, groped on a shelf above the bed for a bottle of Carew's gin and unsteadily slopped some into an enamel mug. He helped himself once more before coming out to shave and deal with another day. Not long afterwards I took a weekend off to visit Guggenheim at Cawnpore and when I returned the Canadian had gone. I heard later that he was in hospital. Mukerji, who took his place, was a small, dark, opinionated Bengali with whom we had long arguments on medical matters. I was unlucky in my tent companions for after some weeks he began to show signs of mental disturbance and was also replaced.

The CO generally joined us for breakfast and might talk about how the training programme was going and tell us of any particular jobs he wanted us to do. It was characteristic of him that on leaving the Mess he took out a flat silver cigarette case, extracted one particular cigarette with great deliberation and carefully tapped the end before lighting it; he then marched away, leather-bound cane firmly under his arm, and broad, flat-rimmed terai hat with handsome puggaree squarely on his head.

Captain Donaldson came from Manchester and had a catholic interest in music, ranging from Bach cantatas to Vera Lynn; the gramophone and the records in the mess were his and he needed a speculative investor's ingenuity and a knowledge of all the storage places in the unit transport to take with him all his comforts when the unit was on the move. He had already been two years in India and in 1943 he had been in one of the unsuccessful Arakan campaigns. In the weeks to come we were to hear many times that no conditions we were called on to endure could measure up to those in the Arakan for humid heat, jungle, insects and the terror of approaching and encircling Japs.

The mornings at 7 IMFTU were given over to training. Don and

I taught the British orderlies, and Terry and the Indian doctors taught the sepoys. The British orderlies had done courses somewhere else on the work of Military Hospitals and Field Ambulances but most of the sepoys, after being given a uniform and being taught to salute and march, had come straight to us from the recruiting depots. They were young and very like friendly children and I enjoyed their company. Sepoys had their own NCOs and VCOs (Viceroy Commissioned Officers). The NCOs (Havildar and Naik) corresponded to our Sergeant and Corporal, but the VCO was a kind of officer unique to the Indian Army, having no exact equivalent in the British Army. He would fit in perhaps somewhere between a junior Warrant Officer and a Subaltern, and there were some who rose to positions very like that of a Regimental Sergeant Major. There were three grades of VCO: Jemadar, Subedar and Subedar Major, and all were addressed 'Sahib'. The IMFTUs had no IOR (Indian Other Rank) senior to Jemadar and no BOR (British Other Rank) as senior as RSM.

We went on route marches in the surrounding country, which was flat and dotted with villages hidden in clumps of trees. The Ganges Plain seemed limitless and as the days and nights grew ever hotter we felt that we should never leave it. The sun rose and set on the plain day after day; its huge beauty was the beauty only of dusk, sunrise and sunset. In between there was only the vast bowl of blue and the heat that pressed down on us and drained us of energy. Distant clumps of trees beyond the dry, infertile foreground made us expect that 'over there' we should find lush pasture, but though we might walk ten miles and more we never did reach it because there was none. In the heat of the day we joined villagers crouching in the shade under mango trees and banyans. Their huts were made of mud-brick and thatch. The poverty was appalling. The holy cow was everywhere.

I enjoyed the route marches. I walked at the back of the column with the senior VCO, Jemadar Nur Mahomet, a well-built man in his thirties with good features, a strong face and a magnificent black moustache which he liked to stroke. He was vain and wore a wonderfully smart felt hat of double thickness like the Gurkhas wore; it was called a 'double terai' and he adorned it with peacock feathers. I wore an ordinary peaked cap.

We marched across small fields of dry earth separated by low earth walls called *bunds*. Cotton or pulse grew sparsely there, and at that season very little else, but birds, including peacock, were plentiful.

I had decided that I must learn Urdu, the lingua franca of the Indian Army; I had bought an Urdu book at the bazaar in Lucknow and had arranged for a teacher or *munshi* to come and teach me for an hour each day. As I walked with Nur Mahomet he gave me language classes of his own. It was hard going at first as he had very little English and I had not got very far with the *munshi*. As we went along Nur Mahomet pointed to birds and beasts and plants and told me their names in Urdu. Progress was painfully slow, but I wrote everything down there and then in a phonetic script of my own. Nur Mahomet used a word *janwar* which puzzled me and shows the sort of question and answer method to which I had to resort. He said one day, pointing as usual;

"That *janwar* is Blue Jay, Sahib," using the Urdu words, and I jumped to the conclusion that *janwar* meant bird, until he pointed to some buffaloes we passed and said, "Those are going-along fellow *janwar*."

Something was wrong and after a moment I tried a question which my small vocabulary allowed: "Jemadar Sahib, is a 'fish' a swimming fellow *janwar*?"

Oh yes, it was, and my guess was right: *janwar* must mean 'animal' or 'creature'. Over a period of weeks I gradually built up my knowledge until a great day came when, doing some job in my tent, I wanted a screwdriver and without thinking called to a passing sepoy to bring me one from the stores. How wonderful! I had used the language and it had worked!

Fairley was older than most of us and had been in general practice in Scotland before he joined up. When I went to his tent I often found him setting up butterflies that he had caught.

"What a pity," he said, "that so many other ranks, and officers too, come out here and find nothing beautiful or interesting. I was overjoyed when I heard I was coming out here."

He already had a considerable collection of butterflies and knew far more than I did about Indian birds. In a wooden cage in his tent he had a pair of blossom-headed parrakeets, called Horace and Irene, which he had bought in the bazaar.

As the weeks went by the heat became more and more

oppressive and after lunch I would often lie on my bed, trying not to listen to what the ornithologist Whistler called the infinitely wearisome cry of the brain-fever bird uttered again and again in a maddening, rising crescendo from a nearby tree. The golden oriole was common in the deserted gardens near our camp; the bird's plumage had a bright metallic glint like that of yellow gold freshly scratched. By our tents Indian crows stalked with mouths wide open, parties of babblers pecked under the bushes, and mynahs and the black and white magpie robin were also common.

In the life we led I was always mentally alone, but at the same time I was in the company of people whose perpetual contact with me interfered with reflection. Only when I was by myself could I begin to think about the future. In my mind was always the image of the great wall to the north, the white snowy barrier I longed to see, and beyond it, in imagination, the distance and immensity of Tibet and China. I could not reconcile these imaginings and longings with a return to a conventional career, with suburban life, a home and marriage with Betty, to whom I was formally and by my own standards firmly tied. I decided that I must sever the link.

One evening as the sun crept down the sky and the welcome shadows touched our tents Kurup invited me to join him. He came from the Malabar coast and had the very black skin of the Dravidian; he was fat, jovial and friendly and the occasional peculiarities of his English were endearing. Once, when we had moved to a place near the Burma border and were talking about religions, he dismissed the subject with, "Oh, in Forward Area all man is God-fearing, is it not?"

He invited me to stay with him after the war in the Malabar States. "I will introduce you to Gandhi-ji." I never knew if he had any special access to Gandhi but such a difficulty would not have occurred to him for a moment when issuing the invitation: the Grand Notion was all and the practicalities nothing. It was the same when I asked him to come with me to Cawnpore for a weekend; he was delighted:

"Oh yes, and we will go on to Benares and visit the shrines."

"O.K. Which way is Benares?"

"Oh, it is the other way."

"Then we can't do it."

"Yes, we can't do it; and also," he smiled broadly, "I do not have the weekend off." But it was a lovely idea. That kind of indulgence in pleasant fantasy must have made many Englishmen think Indians deceitful. To a Welshman perhaps it was easier to understand.

During 1943–4 the British were not popular in India; Gandhi was under house arrest and Nehru and other prominent members of the Congress Party were in gaol. There was still a lot of ill feeling about the Lucknow siege in these parts and we had been warned not to venture alone into the back streets and bazaars of either Cawnpore or Lucknow. I afterwards counted myself lucky that by chance my only postings in India were to two places known to me by stories of what happened there during the Indian Mutiny. Except for Delhi, which I was able to visit later in life, no places were more tragically connected with that uprising, or more able to rouse interest, than Cawnpore and Lucknow.

I made several visits to the old Residency on the bank of the Gumti, where the Union Flag still flew night and day as it had flown since the siege of Lucknow in 1857. It was a curiously vivid encounter with the past: the old guns, the old buildings bearing marks of cannon shot were still there and the atmosphere was overpowering. As a romantic newcomer to India I could very easily conjure up a frightening feeling of being isolated in a great hostile land, of the murdering masses of Oudh and Bihar all around, of fellow-countrymen at Cawnpore slaughtered, of succour impossibly distant, while at my feet the Gumti, flowing to join the Ganges forty miles downstream, was the only link with help, for news in those days could only be sent by hand or heliograph. The relics gave me also an unexpected feeling of pride, a sense that the people who fought here had a link with a part of my past. And mixed with my unease was another feeling – that I must one day come back to this beautiful and hateful land.

By the end of March our training was finished and our newly enlisted ragamuffins had been turned into something like the staff of a field hospital. We dyed our clothes 'jungle green' and gave a few last lectures about camouflage before sending companies of men into the sparse jungle to practise what we thought we had taught them. When Terry and I came to inspect them they proudly showed us tents, lorries and trenches which we had failed to notice and we reflected that concealment might be one thing these children of the jungle did not have to learn from us.

On 5 April we were ready to start for Assam, the forward area where, in Kurup's words, "all man is God-fearing".

The Assam-Burma Border

Between the plains of India and Assam and the central plain of Burma lies a range of wild, jungle covered mountains. It begins at the east end of the Himalayan chain in a tangle of mountain country where no one could have told you where India, Burma, Tibet and China began or ended. From somewhere near Putao, between the Brahmaputra River and the headwaters of the Irrawaddy and Chindwin, the range runs south-west and then south for 500 miles to reach the Bay of Bengal and be lost in the coastal part of Burma known as Arakan.

The mountains, which rise in places to 12,000 feet, have been shaped by erosion and are typically a confusion of high, steepsided ridges separated by deep river valleys. Roads of any kind were then almost non-existent and the region never provided a regular trade route between India and Burma. The rocks are friable and such tracks as were made were always in need of repair.

The climate is like that of tropical rainforest, hot and humid; the annual average rainfall at Cherrapunji in the Khasi hills at the edge of the range is 429 ins. The malaria mosquito is common and the district notorious for the most virulent type of malaria and for tick typhus.

In the middle of the mountains, about halfway between India and Burma, on an oval of flatter ground, stands Imphal, capital of the Indian native state of Manipur. The inhabitants of the little shanty town and its immediate neighbourhood were Manipuris; in the surrounding hills lived a variety of other more or less primitive tribes. Among these were the Nagas to the north and the Chins to the south, both of whom helped us during the war with Japan.

When the Japanese invaded Burma in 1942 it was through those mountains that General Slim brought out what remained of Burma Army, together with thousands of civilian fugitives from the Japanese occupation. The main retreat was by way of the Chindwin and Kabaw Valleys over the mountains to Imphal and thence into Assam and India. Other parties reached Assam by the Hukawng valley and yet others by the Pangsau Pass. Whatever the route, the tracks and weather were atrocious, the suffering great and the dead never counted; there were thousands of them, men, women and children of many races.

During 1943 the Japanese were content to reinforce their armies in Burma and did not attempt any advance in the north; our armies stood on a line east of the mountain chain as far south as the Chin hills. Only in Arakan did the Japanese make a push towards India that year, and with only partial success. They tried again at the beginning of 1944 but were decisively stopped by Slim in February at the battles on and beyond the Ngakeydauk Pass.

In the spring of 1944 the Japanese began to advance in the north with three divisions towards Imphal and the hill village of Kohima, which was strategically placed astride the supply road from Dimapur in Assam. They came from the south through the Chin hills, from the east by the Kabaw Valley and from further north by jungle paths in the Patkai and Naga hills. In the last week of March they surprised the 50th Indian Parachute Brigade at the tiny village of Sangshak, north-east of Imphal, and only took the village after a savage 5-day battle in which there were some 600 casualties on both sides.

By the beginning of April our troops in the Chin hills had been withdrawn to the Imphal plain; units east of Imphal had drawn back to form a defensive ring in the hills round the plain. Non-combatants had been sent down the road to Dimapur, and the fighting troops near Kohima had been formed into a small defensive 'box' at that village. The Japanese were by this time at the edge of the Imphal plain, and to the north Naga scouts had sighted Japanese columns marching along jungle tracks and converging in strength on Kohima.

That was the general military position when Nos. 5 and 7 IMFTU were getting ready to board a train for Assam.

Chapter 4

Assam

"CHARLES, THE SIGNAL'S bloody stuck again." Bill Gleed came lumbering back to our coach, mopping his forehead. He was a big man with a beery belly. He seized the handrails on each side of the steps to the compartment and after hoisting himself up began to fan his face with his bush hat. We were in a railway siding in Bengal and had been there some hours. Our 'special train' for the two IMFTUs sounded grand but meant only that we could be pushed into a siding without warning when more important trains were to pass to the Assam front; we had no timetable and we never knew when we were going to halt or for how long. I shared a four-berth compartment with Wallace Parke and the registrars of the two IMFTUs, Bill Gleed and Usher.

My favourite seat when the train was moving was on the floor in the open doorway, my feet on the step below. There was a cooling breeze here and I could watch the life of the country as we rumbled by at 20 miles an hour. Men were at work in the small fields at dawn, women walked gracefully along the *bunds* with pitchers balanced on their heads. There were groups of villagers shoulder-deep in 'tanks', artificial ponds made of earth and clay; they were fishing with nets or collecting weed from the bottom; they put what they found into pots that floated near them. As we travelled I had a wonderful opportunity to see a huge variety of birds. There were bee-eaters of several kinds on the posts and wires, king-crows with curly forked tails, shrikes, wire-tailed swallows and, on the backs of cattle were crows, egrets and mynahs. The Brahminy kite, a handsome bird of prey with a chestnut body and white head, could be seen perching on posts near water.

It was the year after the Bengal famine of 1943, and in Bihar and

Bengal we saw the effects everywhere: emaciated women, men whose limbs were so thin that I could make out the shape of every bone, families grubbing for scraps in heaps of cinders and rubbish. The children were the worst to see, their arms and legs spindly, their eyes hollow and their bellies big. We wondered naively why people like these had children and why anyone bothered to fight disease in such places. On the train we isolated ourselves from these wretched people; sepoys and British alike, we could not look on them as human; perhaps it was we who were not human.

We passed cities with famous names like Benares where, from a high railway bridge, I saw the river frontage of a thousand temples and below me the burning ghats and the bathing ghats and the multitudes doing homage in the sacred Ganges. We came to big junctions and yards near Calcutta and the stops became longer and more frequent. At all but the briefest of these the IORs walked up the line to the engine, taking large *deckchies* in which they put tea leaves, condensed milk and sugar. The train driver added several gallons of scalding water from the engine boiler; two men were needed to carry back each full *deckchi*. As they passed our carriage we dipped our chipped enamel mugs in the hot sweet, milky brew. Near Calcutta and the delta country there were green coconuts for sale and we drank the milk, but the tea made with engine water was more refreshing.

It was Easter Sunday, 9 April. Kohima and the Imphal plain were under attack and Dimapur threatened. The battles of Imphal and Kohima were soon to be at their height. Not until 18 April was the besieged Kohima garrison at last relieved, and it was to be six more weeks before the battle of the Kohima ridge was won and the road to Imphal was once again open.

On the fourth day the train reached the Brahmaputra at Sirajganj, where a river steamer was moored to the bank. We all went on board, except for those who had gone by road with the transport and heavy gear; they would cross the river farther up at Jogihopa. We spent a day and a night at Sirajganj and slept on board. I set up my bed on deck where I could watch the river. There were permanent cookhouses and mess tents on shore where, at meal times, we lined up with our plates and mugs to collect food and dash for cover before the food was snatched by the kites circling overhead. They were very bold and would swoop down to take the meat off your plate unless you held your hat over it for protection; they seized it with a claw before transferring it to the beak in flight. Corporal Heywood, long-limbed and given to slouching, had carried a pet chameleon in the fold of his bush hat for weeks; it met its fate here for it was snatched by a kite as he walked from the river to the cookhouse.

Sirajganj was a desolate place: there was nothing there except the end of a railway and some tents, sand blowing past, the Brahmaputra rolling by and the far bank so far away as to be barely visible. The river was brown and frothy and the current strong. I could see the backs of creatures I took to be porpoises and learned later that the Brahmaputra and Ganges had their own fresh-water dolphins known as *Susu*. They are sightless and spend their lives grubbing about in the mud on the river bottom – the human lot, I used to think when discontented.

As we got under way I lay by the rail watching the high bank go by, a thin layer of soil above a sandstone cliff. On top of the soil there was a little grass and here and there a tree; a man walked behind a plough drawn by a bullock. I was looking at a cross-section of the earth's crust, and at man clinging with his roots hardly any way into the soil.

River boats passed by, stout craft perhaps 50 feet long with a pointed stem and high bulky stern. There was a mast amidships and aft of it a low bamboo house. For days they drifted quietly downstream with their cargoes until it was time to return; then they were towed up-river by long ropes fixed to the top of the mast, three men walking on the bank, hauling.

On 12 April we turned in to the south bank of the river and disembarked at Pandu where we spent a couple of nights on shore. For the next 200 miles we travelled by train through flat, thickly wooded country which now and then opened up to reveal flood-land and swamp. In one such place I saw a bird about the size and shape of a moorhen walking elegantly and delicately across the leaves which floated on the water; its tail was long and slender and curved like a pheasant's, and its long toes were spread wide to distribute its weight – the pheasant-tailed jacana or lily-trotter.

We reached Dimapur on 16 April and by nightfall were comfortably settled in what were called *bashas*, bamboo dwellings characteristic of Assam; the frame was made of the trunks of bamboo and the walls of bamboo matting. The roof might be made of anything from banana leaves to corrugated iron and the floor was of mud or cement.

Dimapur, also called Manipur Road, was little more than a rough clearing in the jungle, and the only reason for its existence was that it was a convenient point for the transfer from rail to road of goods destined for the hill state of Manipur. The railway passed through on its way to lonely tea gardens beyond Tinsukia in upper Assam, and only a few sidings and sheds marked the unloading place. The whole site had the look of a refuse dump, not improved by the additional clearings and the growth of temporary accommodation needed to supply an army that was to meet the advance of the Japanese through Burma.

The most interesting relic of the past at Dimapur was to be found deep in the forest, a strange collection of megaliths, huge phallic stone pillars of obscure religious significance. It was referred to with relish by the BORs as 'Penis Park'.

5 IMFTU opened first, in tents in a clearing well away from the railway. Soon large numbers of sick were being brought in each day and the MOs of 5 IMFTU were at full stretch. I was told to go there and help Fairley and Dawson with the British patients. I used to walk over (it was about a quarter of a mile) early in the morning and work there until evening when I came back for dinner at my own unit. I enjoyed these walks through luxuriant jungle in the cool of the day and I used to loiter to look at whatever there was to see.

The patients lay in rows on stretchers on the ground in a large marquee-style tent. I began the day by seeing new patients who had come in during the night. I would kneel by the stretchers to question and examine each man and fill in the printed card on which we kept a record. They were usually typical cases of what was euphemistically known as 'Benign Tertian Malaria' – 'feevah'. During the attacks, which came on regularly every other day, the patients felt cold and started to shiver violently until their temperature rose and they broke out in a profuse sweat. When the attacks were over they would get up and walk about listlessly in ill-fitting hospital pyjamas. They were very thin and they looked pale and ill and weak, their skins stained yellow with Mepacrine. Nursing by our male orderlies, when all there was for a bed was a canvas stretcher, was primitive, but at least the patients were being cared for away from the fighting up the road.

I wrote the details of symptoms and examination on the cards, followed by my diagnosis and instructions for treatment. This was carried out by the NCOs and for cases of malaria consisted of regular dosage with pills: quinine, mepacrine (atebrin) and pamaquin; patients were also given a mixture of aspirin, phenacetin and codeine for headaches and other pains. An NCO took blood samples from all new arrivals so that we could look for malaria parasites to confirm the diagnosis. The whole process was regular and mechanical except when a man was unusually ill or suffered from some illness other than malaria.

There was a Field Ambulance near us at Dimapur and the doctors there were also having a busy time because large numbers of battle casualties were being brought down from Kohima, many seriously wounded and some who had had to lie for days in the open.

Our days were full; every stretcher in the tents was occupied, but in the heat of the afternoon Fairley and I would sometimes take a short walk together in the shade of the jungle, which was full of birds. We saw jungle fowl, rather like the ordinary barn-door fowl and we could hear the 'hoo, hoo, hoo' of what I later knew to be the Himalayan cuckoo though we could not find it. Instead, we came on a noisy party of hornbills busy among some low branches – weird caricatures of birds, the heavy bill and casque almost as big as the rest of the body. There were large, beautifully coloured spiders and innumerable insects. The forest was always noisy; there was a continuous low humming made of a thousand sounds that I could not disentangle, and above it those I recognized – the raucous call of jungle fowl, the screeching of magpie-like birds and the monotonous, metallic, unstopping tonk, tonk, tonk of the coppersmith, a shy bird we seldom saw.

On my first day at Dimapur I had been aware of a continuous loud noise like that of a line being drawn steadily off a fishing reel; it was made by the cicada and, like the call of the coppersmith, was never absent from life at Dimapur. It was louder at night and at dusk, and sometimes in the Mess we caught one of these peculiarly ugly insects, of which there were many kinds. One kind we called the Flying Frog; it was about two inches long, with bulging eyes.

One night our CO at 7 IMFTU was sitting on his verandah at dusk; he felt something on the back of his neck and his hand closed on a Flying Frog. He leapt to his feet crying, "God, it's You!" So it (or they, for we usually found more than one a night) became a symbol, a kind of deity. They were One and we knew Him.

One day I went for a walk alone and carelessly lost my way. My sense of direction was soon entirely gone and my only guide an occasional glimpse of the sun through the forest. I was surrounded by the profusion and tangle of the jungle. Huge trees soared up to arch overhead like the pillars of Westminster Abbey; the bark was grey and the lower parts of the trunks spread out in wide, slender supporting branches. I looked up through a framework of hanging aerial roots and trailing creepers to tufts of greenery at the very tops of towering trees. I came on two Assamese who greeted me from a distance by showing their open palms. They carried long knives or *dahs*, broader at the end than near the handle, and they pointed out the way back to Dimapur.

7 IMFTU began to take in patients early in May and my trips to No. 5 ended. For the next four months I was kept busy in our unit. John Wakeford gave me the sick BORs to look after and also put me in charge of the unit dispensary.

Our patients were accommodated in bashas. The larger of these huts, open along one side, were about 30 yards long and eight feet wide, a bit wider than the length of a stretcher; we used these as wards. The MOs slept in a group of small huts near the site entrance and ten yards from our living quarters was a basha we set aside as a clinical laboratory and a ward for the very ill. There were three rooms: in one we put a workbench, microscopes and a few necessary bottles. The second we made into an office for 'Smudger' Smith, the sergeant from South Wales who was in charge of the ward. In the third, which measured about 30 feet by 15, we put folding beds for cases which needed special treatment and constant attention. 'Smudger' was a big, fair young man with a bit too much flesh; he was kind and gentle and he made a very good ward sister. He came to me sometimes to complain when the work was a bit too much for him. Talking about it helped and though our relationship was not very military it was good for the patients.

Not far away but isolated from other buildings was the unit dispensary, a small basha about 10 feet by six. A padlock could be hung on the door for the sake of appearances, but the 'window' of the basha was merely an opening with a flap and a thief could easily have got in. To help me run the dispensary I was given a small dark assistant called Mohammed Aziz who knew absolutely nothing about medicines. I sat down to recall what I had been taught of pharmacy and dispensing at Oxford, but not everything had been taught there and some things I had to learn as I went along. I was in the habit of mixing Gum Arabic with the powdered aspirin, phenacetin and caffeine used to make pain killer for the patients. When I had a bucketful of the thick white mixture I dispensed it in bottles to the various wards; nearing the bottom of the first bucket I realized that there was something more here than the mixture I was doling out, and by and by came first to the tail and then to the remainder of a decomposing rat. No one was any the worse for the rich mixture.

Acting unpaid Lance Naik (L/Cpl) Mohammed Aziz had a sharp little face and never did any grousing; I gradually got to like him and to depend on him. When he joined me he could not write the letters of the English alphabet correctly. I taught him very little, for my knowledge of Urdu was elementary but in two months, by watching everything I did, he learned to run the dispensary on his own. He remembered the amounts for making up stock medicines, he weighed carefully, and he was honest. I normally directed what he did but when I was ill and once when I was away for more than a week I trusted him completely with the routine work and he did not let me down. To pick up all this from a foreigner who did not speak his language properly, in a subject about which, to begin with, he knew nothing, argued a good and adaptable mind.

To Mohammed Aziz all the technical words were strange and he invented his own romanized spellings for the sounds: for instance 'miss pock sick' for mist. pot. cit. (potassium citrate mixture) and 'miss sline' for mist. saline. (saline mixture).

Hari Shankar, the batman I shared with the CO, was by contrast shy, awkward and much less intelligent; he was not slow to pick up ideas but he did not get them right. He had difficulty in grasping simple mechanical principles which would not have bothered Mohammed Aziz for a moment, and he had no sense of proportion or of priorities. A practical job would be forgotten because an artistic notion presented itself and he would devote hours to small unimportant tasks. I had asked him to make a mud wall inside my tent to direct the rain out, and he built it outside so that the water was directed in. I had a trench outside the tent to drain away the water which fell heavily each night, and he filled part of this useful drain with soil so that he could plant flowers on each side of the entrance. He then built two low walls from my doorway for a few yards and planted them also with flowers, but there was still no wall inside the tent to keep the floor dry. I put up with much of this because Hari Shankar was doing his best and, as Kurup was fond of saying, 'You do not want clever man as servant; you want man who loves you.' After ironing the CO's drill trousers with too hot an iron and burning holes in the material, Hari Shankar made the mistake of trying to hide the black patches by cutting them away with scissors. The solution was too simple and he had to go.

My next batman, Sadheo, had a pale, lightly pockmarked skin, pronounced Tibeto-Burman features and a thin but definite moustache; he was extraordinarily stupid. He came from a village under Dhaolagiri, one of the great peaks of the Nepal Himalaya. Many of the Gurkhas were recruited from that part of Nepal, but I suspect that Sadheo was too stupid for the Gurkhas. We had no common language but remained, as far as I could tell, on friendly terms, though I was never able to make head or tail of what he said. He tried hard to make me understand, as a last resort by shouting; then he would see that it was no use because I still didn't understand, or perhaps could not hear, and we would both grin like hell. He was extremely lazy and rather cunning; he had various treasures such as a 'swagger cane' with a bit of silver on the end, and because it was not safe in his kit he used to hide it by day in my bed, something I discovered by happening to sit on it. He liked heavily scented hair-oil and hid the bottles in my boots. He smoked *ganja* (Indian hemp) a great deal and in the end he became so useless that, likeable or not, I had to sack him too. It was an unhappy end for him because an officer's batman had various perks and escaped many irksome duties.

Work on the wards at 7 IMFTU was like that at No. 5 except

that sometimes the colonel came round with me. He noticed at once the number of regular takers of mepacrine who were nevertheless down with first attacks of malaria, and we wondered how regular their taking of mepacrine had really been in the circumstances of their life 'up the road', and under the insidious influence of tales that these tablets that made you yellow also made you impotent.

We took mosquitoes very seriously. XIVth Army orders were: 'shirt sleeves rolled down and trousers tucked into socks after sundown', and everyone in static camps like ours slept under mosquito nets, as did the patients on their stretchers. Wide deep drains had been cut through the site to clear away standing water and lessen the number of breeding places for mosquitoes, and there was a daily morning routine to keep down mosquitoes in the camp. My day started before dawn with the arrival of the 'FLIT SQUAD'; the party, headed by some kind of NCO, invaded my bedroom before I was up. They were funny little barefoot ragamuffins in dirty vests and shorts who smoked cigarettes as fast as they could light them. All were armed with flit guns and went round buildings and tents spraying inside every corner and shaded spot.

Running the dispensary gave me a reason to visit the Base Depot Medical Stores a few miles out past Dimapur bazaar on the Nichugard road. On either side was what they called 'partially exploited jungle', which had been cleared in a patchy way for cultivation. I saw tree orchids, plumbago in flower and the heavy sweet flowers of frangipani. There was a stream of military traffic going to and from Kohima – mule trains, trucks, ambulances, jeeps. The road was busy too with pedestrians coming and going between the hills and Dimapur and we passed gangs of coolies carrying mattocks and hoes and wearing wide-brimmed bamboo hats.

Most interesting were the Nagas who had come down from the mountains. They were stocky folk, a rich chocolate colour, with black hair worn long or cut in 'pudding-basin' style. They had great muscular calves and thighs, almond eyes and chubby faces. Although we were very interested in them they looked through us as though we did not exist. They wore black blankets with red, gold, white and green stripes along the edge. The men wore a black cloth band round the leg just below the knee, and often a gold bangle as well. They had necklaces of bright red beads and some wore crimson scarves. On their backs they carried bamboo wicker baskets, using head straps. Their faces were full of life, the men grave, the boys ready to smile back, and the girls attractive to look at. They were wild, wary creatures, at home in that savage country; they would tolerate our passage and still be there with the rain and the jungle when the brief disturbance we caused had passed.

The Nagas were the happiest looking folk I had seen. The Indians I encountered often had a depressed, downcast look in spite of their festivities and dancing; perhaps they thought too much. "If you are of an enquiring mind it is difficult to be happy," as Guggenheim used to say.

I had a steady stream of visitors at the dispensary: cadgers, grousers and sometimes men who just wanted conversation or who wanted to show me a new bird or beast which might interest me.

Mac, the lieutenant QM, came one morning and began, "I've been in the army all my life, Charles, and I know the form about these things." I knew the form too by then: he was after my store of brandy (known as medical comforts). He had a fearful Irish temper which exploded suddenly and blew over as quickly; then he was all smiles. He liked literature and especially admired Shakespeare, Hardy, Milton and the Bible: "Foine English it is, though mind you I'm not religious at all at all." I never caught him reading any of them.

When the Stores Jemadar called, his object, after telling me how well I was liked and many other things, was to get quinine from me, for quinine was in short supply and could be sold. He tried to ingratiate himself by passing on natural history notes, "Sahib, look, very bad snake in tree: he make noise at night."

"But it's got legs, Jemadar Sahib."

"Oh yes, Sahib, snake have got legs."

The only snake killed in camp that was brought to me was small, about two feet long, and had pairs of narrow rings all the way down its body. I thought it might be a krait which would indeed have been 'very bad', but its head was too crushed for me to be sure. The IOR who brought it said it was 'very bad snake', but I never came across a snake that was not very bad to the uneducated.

The BORs complained too, and sometimes I felt that my job was to be a sponge that mopped up everybody's grouse, and that the grousing cured them. One BOR brought me a furry brown spider two and a half inches long and half an inch wide. Another brought me an insect like a grasshopper, about 2½ inches long; when its wings were closed over its back it looked like a piece of bark.

Insects were always attracted to our dinner table by the powerful light of the Petromax lamps we used. Praying mantis 3 inches long often landed on the tablecloth and their dancing and gesticulating antics distracted us from our usual occupation of scooping from the soup the discarded wings of flying ants.

One evening after a five course dinner made from whatever our cook could find in the rations we sat out under the stars in deck chairs, smoking long thin cigars from Madras and watching the fireflies against the black night. We were suddenly roused by hearing on the radio the word 'Dimapur': it was, it seemed, a 'remote railhead in a jungle hell'.

We listened to the radio on most nights and the announcement on 6 June of landings in Normandy affected us all profoundly. At last the end was in sight; personal problems appeared in a different light and we wondered if any of our friends were now in the thick of it in France. On 16 June we heard, "Japanese mainland bombed yesterday by land-based aircraft," another milestone. And on the 29th, as light relief, we heard on a Japanese-controlled English-language broadcast from Saigon that "Nothing could now stop the victorious march on Delhi of our triumphant Japanese armies." We knew that it was a week since the road from Dimapur to Imphal had finally been cleared of Japs by the 2nd British and 5th

Indian Divisions; any threat to Delhi was now over. On another night I tuned in by chance to a German radio programme and heard the Brandenburg Concerto No. 5; it did not come through very well but it was utterly transporting.

The BBC was right about the climate. From the time we came to Dimapur until the middle of July the minimum temperature was never below 75 degrees F. and there were nights in mid-June when the minimum temperature was 97 degrees. Humidity varied from 75% to 98%, and 98% was not uncommon. When I dissolved carbolic crystals in water early in the morning to make calamine lotion, the drops of moisture that condensed on the outside of the beaker ran down the glass and made a pool on the table.

Thunderstorms were frequent after the beginning of May and on one night we had a particularly violent electric storm. First the wind whirled a few sheets of metal and an old tarpaulin through the camp. Then came the first drops of rain, the crash of a chair blown over, and the first clear blue startling flashes of lightning. We hurried to rescue our possessions; Don got his gramophone into his basha and I took down my mosquito net which was flapping like a loose-footed sail and dragged my bed into Don's basha. He had put on a record from Peer Gynt. The storm, he said, reminded him of just such a night last year in the Arakan, when he was waiting in the dark for the return of his companions. In between flashes I could still see on my retina the images of another basha and of a great tree against the sky. Then the whole place was brilliantly lit again and the tree and basha were momentary black silhouettes. Rain streaked across these fleeting visions and drummed loudly on the ground, steady and unceasing.

The moist heat sapped our energy and we grew ill-tempered. I seemed with everyone to have to be saying to myself, "Don't shout at him" and I remembered Kurup's complacent self-praise, "But I do not hit the patients".

I was watching a golden oriole one morning when Smudger, who was not very observant, came to the dispensary and remarked, "No birds around here Sir, like there is at home. Just drab sparrows and things." He must have been feeling the heat for a moment later he exclaimed in front of a harmless little sepoy, "Christ, I hate this chap!" Later, in the Mess I was irritated when

Bill Gleed and Don began talking about pacifists. I did not want to get drawn into a discussion started by Don with the words, "Of course, 95% of all Conscientious Objectors are just trying to get out of it." I remembered the pressures put on me as a boy and the embarrassment of being taken by my family to listen to the pacifist George Lansbury, a man I did not find sympathetic. I had known plenty of pacifists and most of them had dropped their pacifism when war began.

In the hot weather I finally lost my temper with Mukerji when he failed to turn up on the second day running for a Health Inspection of the IORs which he was due to take. I found him in bed pretending that the job was for me to do. Another argument with Mukerji began when he announced that sodium salicylate "toned up the liver cells".

"What evidence is there that it tones up the liver cells?"

"It's in the book."

"Yes, I know, but the book may be wrong. What is the evidence for what is in the book?"

"What do you mean, evidence? Pharmacopoeia says it."

I laughed at him: my medical school had bred scepticism about this sort of thing.

When Mukerji, who suffered from moodiness, sent a message to say that he did not intend to come to Terry's birthday celebration, Kurup, always good-natured, said, "Oh he is silly fellow," and added with a broad smile, "So he has buttered his bread, so he must lie on it. Is it not?" Not long afterwards Mukerji went mad and was removed.

Convalescents who had recovered enough to walk used a large tent as a Mess where they had their meals and played housey-housey; occasionally on fine nights there were film shows under the stars. Vera Lynn came to see us, wearing a wide-brimmed bush hat, bush shirt and slacks; she did a great deal of good by going round and talking to the men. She spent time with the convalescents and her visit was treasured. I suppose she sang but I did not remember it. Just seeing her and hearing her speak was enough to make us imagine all sorts of things.

June the twelfth was our hottest day yet. In the small ward for those specially ill was a man with a temperature of 106.5 degrees. Smudger saw to it that he had a proper bed to lie on and was sponged down at intervals. The unhappy man gave a very good picture of what bad malaria could look like – tremendous rigors, temperature soaring, copious sweating which lowered the fever a little, then more shivering and the fever rising once more until there was clouding of consciousness and delirium; we gave him intravenous quinine. When we looked at the blood slides we found the parasites of malignant tertian malaria, 'Damn bad feevah'.

Normally any excuse to be away from Dimapur for a few days would have been welcome, but not when I was ordered to India to attend a Court of Inquiry into the collapse and sudden death of a patient which had occurred while I was operating on him in Cawnpore. John Wakeford, to whom I told the story, said, "Tell them about it like you told me and don't worry. You were doing your best."

I went by rail to Jorhat and was given a lift to Delhi in an American supply plane; I had never flown before. I sat on a heap of sacks in the empty fuselage where I could look out of the window on the starboard side. Soon I was admiring an enormous mass of snow-white cumulus cloud to the north. As time passed it began to look less like cloud and I realized that I was looking at a gigantic range of mountains. I had never seen anything like it. I took out a notebook and made a sketch which I afterwards recognized as the outline of Kanchenjunga, Kabru and Jannu.

At Cawnpore a Lieutenant-Colonel and two officers sat at a bare table; I saluted and was invited to sit in front of them. The Colonel suggested that I should give an account of what had happened. I fixed my gaze on a fly that buzzed about the Colonel's nose as I told the story:

"The patient had been ill for a long time and we had been unable to make a diagnosis or decide on treatment. We needed to look at a bit of bone marrow under a microscope and in getting the specimen from his breast-bone my needle had gone too deep and had scratched the surface of his heart. We knew afterwards that there had been a tear and a haemorrhage into the sac in which the heart lies. Yes, the needle was unprotected, but it was the only kind we had in that hospital.

"Yes, I had done that sort of thing before, but using safe needles with a short bevel and a safety collar. Yes, I had had to push to reach the marrow in the breast-bone, and yes, the push had gone that little bit too far. Yes, every precaution had been taken except to transfer the patient somewhere where they had the proper tools."

So we went on until my tale was told and they called the next witness. He was a doctor who had suggested that there was no need for a post mortem examination: I was glad now that I had disagreed with him. We should never have known the truth without that anxious hour of searching in the dead man's body.

Before I left the Court of Inquiry I signed my statement and several days later the Court decided that there had been a 'misadventure' and that no one was guilty of negligence.

A Brigadier Crosbie, RAMC (DDMS 33 Corps) came in unobtrusively one day to have a talk with John Wakeford. We hoped they were discussing a move forward from Dimapur. The CO called me over next day and said he was going for the day to Kohima; would I like to go? I was so excited that I might have been at home going for a day out in the hills. We started at 1130 in a 15-cwt truck; Wakeford sat in front with the driver and I sat in the open back.

First we went through a jungly gorge, then there was a long climb of 5,000 feet, the road twisting and turning along steep hillsides. Landslides were frequent and in one place we came across a bulldozer pushing debris over a steep drop on the outer side of the road. Above and below there was thick jungle except where there had been landslips. Now and then, hundreds of feet down, I could see wrecked 3-tonners whose drivers had gone over the edge. The road was busy with trucks and mule trains. Gangs of coolies from tea gardens were at work with picks, mattocks and shovels, clearing, making passing places and repairing damage. For most of the way we were in low gear, the driver steadily winding the steering wheel as we rounded bend after bend. After 3,000 feet we reached an undulating plateau where there were clearings. The traffic was heavy, mainly 15-cwt trucks, and all along the road Nagas were coming and going.

If I had known more then about the Battle of Kohima I should have looked about me with more care at the slit trenches, old strong points and the tumbledown remains of bunkers, all empty now. Shattered tree trunks, blasted by mortar bombs and shell-

1. The author as a Lieutenant...

2. ...and as a Captain.

3. View East from Fort White, Chin Hills.

4. Termite Hill, Kalemyo.

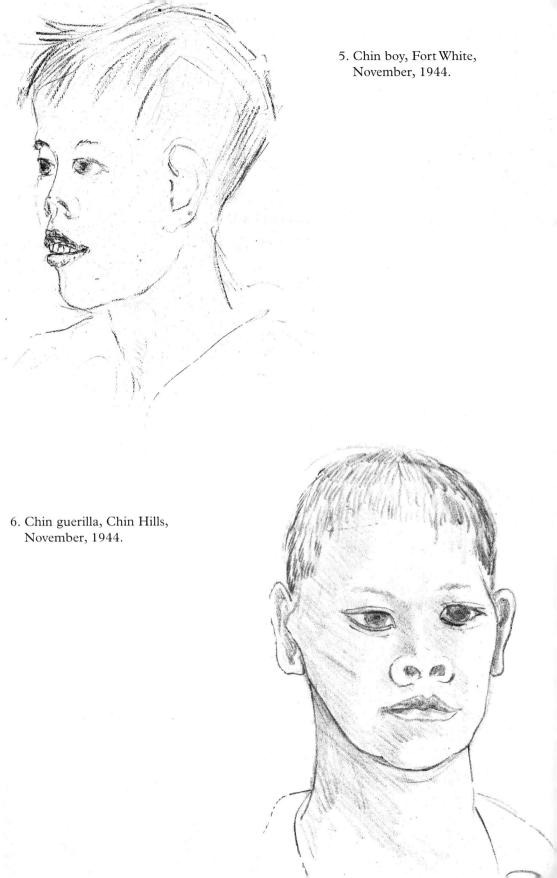

5. Chin boy, Fort White,
   November, 1944.

6. Chin guerilla, Chin Hills,
   November, 1944.

7. Lieutenant Terry, "a sallow young man in the Indian Army Medical Corps" (p.32). He is imitating a ganja smoker.

8. Smudger Smith, "a big, fair young man with a bit too much flesh" (p.45).

fire, bare of branches and leaves, stood out against the sky. West of the road were the remains of shelled buildings, Garrison Hill, a scene of devastation.

8 IMFTU had set up camp east of the road. Near the various hutments which made up the 'native village' stood a neat bungalow with a corrugated iron roof painted red. Somehow it had escaped serious damage. The small garden of roses and bougainvillea was almost intact. We were given tea by a Sikh MO; refreshed by a cool breeze we looked out over the Jessami track to the complicated hills and valleys which opened to the south-east.

At the beginning of September Terry and I went with Kurup to a 'South Indian dinner' in the Travancore lines. There was rice, of course, but also coconut chutney, something called *Idaly*, red stuff called *Sambha* which took the skin off my tongue, and little red balls of fried meat, ladies' fingers, *papar* and ground coconut. The meal was washed down with sweet milky coffee. All joined in and overate grossly, and the atmosphere was fun and laughter. Finally Kurup, our host, stood on his head and explained that this was yoga. "It is," he said, "most difficult one," and as he had a full stomach and stayed upside down for a full minute, or perhaps two, I believed him.

On 8 September we loaded 7 IMFTU into 3-ton trucks; the work took all day and it was nightfall when the last lorries moved off one by one and disappeared up the road into blackness.

Chapter 5

The Central Front

THE ROAD CLIMBED 5,000 feet from Dimapur to Kohima, 46 miles away, the administrative headquarters of the Naga Hills where, before the war, were a 'native village', a Deputy Commissioner's bungalow, and some administrative and military buildings. South of Kohima the road climbed nearly another 1,000 feet before beginning the 3 to 4,000 foot descent into the Imphal plain, which was surrounded on all sides by mountains. These, before the battles for Imphal, had been covered in jungle to their summits. The little collection of villages that made up Imphal, 130 miles from Dimapur, was given strategic importance in 1944 by its geographical position between Burma and India.

From Imphal a bridle path ran south-east over the mountains to the village of Tamu on the India-Burma frontier. Tamu was at the head of the Kabaw Valley, separated from the River Chindwin to the east by a range of low hills. The Tamu track was used by most of those who fled from Burma in 1942.

Another track, longer and rougher than that to Tamu, ran south from Imphal through the Chin hills to a tiny village called Tiddim, 162 miles away in Burma. This was the route followed later by 7 IMFTU.

In 1943–4 the three Indian divisions of 4 Corps occupied the country described: the 23rd Division was at Imphal, the 20th was near Tamu and the 17th Light Division was at Tiddim. Except for some small outposts east of Kohima and north-east of Imphal the other troops in the area were non-combatant. A General Hospital had been brought to Imphal itself and various Line of Communication units were stationed between Dimapur and Imphal.

A good deal of time and labour were devoted in 1943 to

improving the road from Dimapur, but communications by land were generally difficult in the mountains. Communications by air were slightly easier, for by 1944 there were five landing strips at Imphal; only two of these, however, could be used in the rainy season.

Early in 1944 the Japanese began an offensive from the south-east and east, threatening the Imphal plain and its supply line from India via Dimapur. To meet the threat all available major units were withdrawn towards Imphal and formed a defensive ring round the plain; small outlying units were withdrawn to guard the road at Kohima and the British 2nd Division was brought into Assam.

Before the end of March the Battle of Sangshak mentioned earlier had been fought, an important but forgotten battle in which the 50th Indian Parachute Brigade, with no previous experience of battle, delayed the advance of a Japanese division for five vital days.

Meanwhile, to strengthen the defence of Imphal, Slim flew the 5th Indian Division from Arakan – guns, jeeps, mules and all; two brigades of the division went direct to Imphal and one (known as Daddy Warren's) went to Dimapur; that brigade included the 1st Battalion of the Royal West Kents which was immediately to distinguish itself at the siege of Kohima. Slim further reinforced the Central Front by bringing the British 2nd Division from India. When Warren's brigade had raised the siege of Kohima it was the British 2nd Division that took over the battle and cleared the Japanese from the road south.

When 5 and 7 IMFTUs settled in at Dimapur in mid-April the battles for the Imphal plain were at their height and that for Kohima, which began on the night of 3 April, had reached a crucial stage; the small garrison had withstood close and fierce attack for two and a half weeks and was near the end of its endurance. Relief came on 20 April, but although the danger of the Japanese descending on Assam and Dimapur was removed, it was not until two months later that the enemy was cleared from the road to Imphal and troops of the British 2nd Division met troops of the 5th Indian Division advancing north.

To the east and south of the Imphal plain the defenders held their positions from spring to summer and all the Japanese attempts to break into the ring were beaten.

After July the exceptional rains of 1944 turned dripping hill-sides into quagmires and tracks became runnels of mud and clay. The enemy was in retreat, short of supplies, and weakened by disease and starvation. Slim harried him with an army that did not halt for the monsoon, but chased him east to Tamu and the Kabaw valley, and south through the Chin hills to Tiddim and Kalemyo.

Before the war Tiddim had been an outpost of a district of Burma; it consisted of a few dwellings with red tin roofs among scattered hamlets in remote mountainous country. It was approached from Burma by a pack trail that wound up from Kalemyo through towering forests of magnificent teak. The trail had some historic interest for on it was the site of Fort White, named after Sir George White, VC, defender of Ladysmith. As a young brigadier in Burma he had earned the thanks of the Government of India for 'putting down the dacoits and pacifying the country'. If the story is true he must be the only man ever to have done this to Burma, before or since.

Tiddim and the trail from Kalemyo and Fort White over Kennedy Peak became important in 1944 when the Japanese chose it as one route to Manipur. They drove north from Tiddim over the formidable Manipur River while the 17th Indian Light Division, which had been occupying the Chin hills, withdrew in haste and with great difficulty to join in the defence of Imphal. The Japanese advance from the south was halted by troops of 4 Corps at Bishenpur on the southern rim of the Imphal plain and the defeated enemy was forced back the way it had come.

To clear the Chin hills Slim chose the 5th Indian Division which had already fought the axis in Eritrea and the Western Desert and had faced the Japanese in Arakan.

To meet the special circumstances created by the season and the nature of the country a number of units not normally under divisional command were attached to the division; amongst these, seconded from 33 Corps, were 7 IMFTU and a Casualty Clearing Station.

By the beginning of September the 5th Indian Division had advanced 40 miles from the Imphal plain along the Tiddim road and won command of the mountains and jungles on either side.

The main natural obstacle on the way to Tiddim was the Manipur river. It rises in the Imphal plain and flows south until it is about 120 miles from Imphal and 36 miles from Tiddim. Here it bends to the right to run roughly west for half a mile before turning south again. At the bends it is already a big river, wide and swift. The road south from Imphal at first lies west of the river, which is on the driver's left; it reaches the river at mile 126, where traffic must cross it before climbing to Tiddim. After the crossing the river is on the driver's right. There was once a substantial bridge at the crossing but 17th Indian Light Division destroyed it during their retreat in 1944 and although the Japanese must have put up some sort of bridge for their own use they did not leave it intact, and the crossing was a serious obstacle. After the 5th Indian Division crossed the river communication with Imphal by land was cut off and all supplies came by airdrop.

The later course of the Manipur River is south and east through the Chin hills to form the Myittha River, which flows into the Chindwin at Kalewa.

The greater part of the 162 miles from Imphal at 2,000 ft to Tiddim at 5,000 ft was fit only for 'fair-weather' travel. With the passage of a division in the monsoon it became a muddy, deeply rutted scar on which even four-wheel drive vehicles were constantly skidding and slipping; they advanced in crab-like fashion, all wheels turning all the time and the front wheels usually pointing in at an angle to the hillside.

Chapter 6

The Tiddim Road

ON 9 SEPTEMBER Terry and I started for Imphal at daybreak. I climbed into the cab of the 15 cwt Chev and sat with the driver; Terry and his batman got in behind and lay on the baggage. As we passed Dimapur station we heard a shout. It was *Naik* (Corporal) Sita Ram, returned from leave. He threw his gear in the back of the truck and climbed in after it. He and Terry began to converse in fluent Hindi.

   After the first few miles on the flat the road began to climb, one hairpin bend after another. Always on one side there was the steep rising slope and on the other a precipitous drop. After Kohima we climbed for another thousand feet to the highest point on the road, about 5,500 ft. We passed groups of Nagas wearing hats made of bamboo and leaves; the men had grass capes and the women and children carried bamboo baskets on their backs. As we passed they withdrew to the roadside and stood immobile like statues. It rained heavily most of the way and I smoked Woodbines one after another. Near the highest point we stopped to eat a tin of salmon and drink tea from a thermos flask.

In the Imphal plain at 2,000 ft the country was more open; the road crossed shallow, stony streams flanked by grass and trees – the country looked more like home than anything I had seen in the East, but the grass was coarse and more yellow than green, and the woods were wild and tangled. Here and there were patches of brighter green, the fresh young paddy. We reached Imphal an hour before dark and camped on an airfield that was out of use because of the monsoon. We had come 135 miles in under ten hours – good going.

The CO, with Bill Gleed and Wallace Parke, arrived later and we all settled in a corner of a large tent for the night, which was comfortable except for the mosquitoes; even through nets the mosquitoes of Imphal had sudden stabbing bites that one did not forget. I rose early and went up the highest of a ring of hills near camp. The lower slopes were covered with scrub; conifers and elephant grass grew on the top, where I found the remains of a strongpoint and trenches, and from which I looked down on the whole Imphal plain; we were not far from the centre of it.

We stayed at Imphal only to be sure that the unit was together before starting along the Tiddim road in the wake of the 5th Indian Division. The CO and I left at 0800 on 11 September with two of the office clerks, Muthu Krishnan and Ram Chandar. At first the road was good. We passed an all-weather (tar macadam) airfield and came to Bishenpur, the village at the south end of the plain where one of the notable battles of the siege of Imphal had taken place. After mile 30 (the miles were marked with wooden posts) the road began to deteriorate as it climbed into the mountains; we passed wrecked tanks, Japanese remains and the burnt-out wrecks of lorries. We admired the engineers who had made this road: we did not know what was yet to come. We churned slowly through mud, all four wheels spinning in deep ruts; at mile 43 we stopped for a break and had lunch. We entered Burma at mile 75; but for the map we should not have known it.

Small white crosses marked our soldiers' graves and an occasional Jap skull grinned at us from the side of the track where some joker had stuck it on a post. At mile 80.5, near the tents of a Field Ambulance, we stopped to set up our own camp. We were going to be here for the next two and a half weeks, to the end of September. The site was in partly cleared jungle near a bend in a pleasant stream about 20 yards broad; the water was clear and deep enough for swimming and I went in at once to wash off the dust of the journey. Around us now were decomposing Japanese dead, unexploded grenades, discarded clips of ammunition and flies in abundance. On the far side of the road, not fifty yards away, an abandoned ammunition dump was on fire.

It rained heavily all the first day but a party of our convoy of trucks arrived before nightfall: we could put up tents and begin to take in patients. Several British patients appeared and with a hurricane lamp in my hand and a gas cape over my head I went across the camp to attend to them. On the way back to the Mess in the dark and rain I fell into a hole full of mud and reached the mess tent in no mood to be told that the cooks had gone to bed. Terry had been out to see sick Indian troops and the two of us ate what we could find in tins in the deserted cookhouse.

New patients came in all day and the British section was soon full. Heavy and continuous rain fell day and night: the river where I liked to swim each morning became a torrent sweeping violently downstream into a noisy gorge; tree trunks, petrol cans and all sorts of rubbish came down it. Engineers farther along the road were trying to rig a cable ferry over the Manipur River, and in one night measured a rise of three feet in river level and an increase in the rate of the current to 16 knots.

At lunch one day Bill Gleed announced that as I had been a year in the army I was now a Captain: he had received formal notice of the fact. The announcement was greeted with enthusiasm by all because it was an excuse for a party and the QM was expected to provide the means of celebrating; we had all long since finished the month's ration of drink. Mac later privately passed me a bottle of Canadian Club and with the addition of rum we had a good evening.

Next day I went up one of the hills above camp; it was honey-combed with bunkers in which were Japanese sandals, tin hats and water bottles, and a litter of corncobs gnawed down to the wood. I met two Chins on my walk and was sorry that we had no common language. Their bearing and the way they looked through me as if I was not there gave me a chastening feeling of being a mere object like a stone or tree in the landscape. They had broader, shorter *dahs* than the Nagas and to carry the panniers on their backs they used plaited headropes; these passed through holes in yokes made of polished red-brown wood that looked like mahogany. The ropes were knotted so that the yoke took some of the weight off the fore-head. On the way back I stopped by a mound at the side of the track, idly stirring it with the toe of my boot. I exposed a number of bodies, scraps of uniform and toothy Jap skulls; the bones were yellowed, the eye sockets huge.

Malaria could strike very quickly. On 20 September I recorded that a British soldier lost consciousness at 1300 and was dead at 1530. He had his first symptoms the previous day and in the morning was outwardly no different from many other patients. Wallace Parke and I wondered if his death could be from some other cause than malaria and I did a post mortem examination in a small tent: we had the necessary tools in our stores. When I took off the top of the skull I found the brain very much congested with blood and when we looked at sections we found it to be full of malaria parasites. There was no sign of any other cause of death.

On 26 September a Casualty Clearing Station arrived and set up camp near us, complete with specialists, operating theatre, nurses, pet dogs, everything; some of them joined us as guests for dinner. Our mess tent was pitched on a steep slope and during meals Bill and Mac were in the habit of sharing a wooden bench which ran along the side of the tent that was over the slope to the river. That night at dinner we turned on the radio to hear the news and were surprised to hear a tribute paid to the Indian Army. Bill had had a drink or two with our guests and struggled to his feet to wave his glass in acknowledgement; when he sat down heavily he and Mac disappeared backwards with a noise of splintering wood – out of the tent and into the dark. We helped them back to the table and when the guests had gone we finished what the QM said was the last of the spirits. Next night, when I joined the sergeants for a

63

beer, a bottle of rum appeared; the label said 'Lime Juice' and Smudger murmured, "Funny, that. The QM must have overlooked it, Sir."

About this time there was some question about taking nursing sisters any farther. After crossing the Manipur River the road back would be allowed to fall into disrepair; we should be cut off behind and supplied only by airdrop. Some people remembered the capture of a Main Dressing Station in Arakan when the Japs murdered the staff and patients. They did not think any girls should go on, but so many volunteered that it was difficult to leave even one behind.

The CCS had on the staff a young doctor called Klein who fancied himself as a psychiatrist. He joined us for dinner one evening and after a silence suddenly turned to me and asked, "Do you like painting, Evans?"

When I cautiously answered, "Yes" he immediately asked, "What?"

"Oh, not modern stuff."

"You disappoint me."

He wanted me to know that he made a study of the Pre-Raphaelites and Post-Impressionists, and of Surrealism. I told him that I liked well drawn pictures of subjects I could recognize and added for good measure that I liked to read Milton. He sniffed a bit and moved on to music – Debussy and Sibelius. Somehow he seemed familiar, but we had not met: it was the opinions and phrases that were boringly familiar.

"Any single man over forty has a fundamental psychological defect."

"All Indians, you know, have complexes which make them aggressive."

"Mountaineering? A thwarted desire, of course, to get above your fellows."

I demurred and he retreated. "Oh, my dear chap, don't think I meant to be personal."

He could make nothing, he said, of Colonel Wakeford; it occurred to me that John Wakeford thoroughly understood Klein.

In the last week of September we had orders to pack and be ready to move; soon there were no patients and we had time on our hands. The river level had fallen and I tried fishing but although I had the right gear, proper hooks and fishing line, I caught nothing, whereas our Indian cook regularly caught fish for our meals with a bent pin and a piece of cotton. I saw snakes now and then at the pool, either swimming or on the stones by the water; as far as I knew they were harmless. Chestnut-headed bee-eaters with bright plumage perched on the trees.

Half the unit, including the CO and the QM, now left to go farther along the road while I stayed with Bill Gleed, Kurup and various NCOs. I fetched my revolver and got Bill to dig out a rifle. After I had found out that I was not much good with the revolver I got Bill to show me over the rifle; it was the ordinary Lee-Enfield .303 and as I was accustomed to sporting guns I had no difficulty with it when we started target shooting.

From that time Bill Gleed and Smudger Smith and I struck up friendships that were to last as long as we were together. There was a surprising amount of drink in the sergeants' tents and I began to see that Bill's relations with the NCOs were on a much more intimate footing than Mac's had been. It was at Smudger's invitation that Bill and I went to the Sergeants' Mess that night to finish what was left of the QM's whisky.

A Field Park Company of Indian Engineers was camped two miles up the road and next evening a tall slim Cockney sergeant called Barney came in a jeep to fetch us to a party with them. Two of our sergeants, Vedmore and Edwards, piled in with Smudger, Bill and me and we bucketed along the road. The engineers fed us on fresh chicken from a Chin village followed by peaches out of a tin; then, round a fire in the open, we played a simplified version of poker till the small hours.

We moved on on 1 October, travelling in convoy. First we followed a river at the bottom of a deep gorge; then, traversing steep, crumbling slopes and winding in and out of small ravines, we climbed the side of the gorge to a saddle. We then went along a high ridge with glorious views of sun and mist on distant ranges before plunging dizzily down hairpin bends into the next gorge. The road was just passable, one mile per gallon, 6 to 20 miles per day, depending on landslips and other obstructions like stranded vehicles. I rode with Smudger and two others in the back of a 3-ton truck, lying on folded tents. At milestone 87 the road climbed across a particularly steep slope where tarpaulins were draped above and below to stabilize the soil. This was known as 'The Ladder' and the track there was no more than a narrow ledge cut along the side of a mountain of mud and shale. We halted at a point where the road rounded a sharp edge and to one side there was a great drop. Because of the fumes in the covered truck, we had splitting headaches. Smudger and a havildar called Malachi got out and were violently sick. It was near noon and blazing hot; I got out of the truck to bandage the septic hand of an engineer lieutenant who was standing by the road and I passed out. I remembered the fight to keep bandaging though my hands were fumbling, the spasm of fear, "Christ! Is it M.T. (Malignant Tertian malaria)?", then the glorious cool surrender as I was carried to the roadside. At that moment I was coming round and told someone to put me with my head down. He covered my face from the sun and in a few minutes I was all right. At last we got to milestone 100 and stopped for the night – 20 miles. Very good going, we were told.

We went on in the morning at 0900 and made good progress with no long halts, reaching milestone 126 at 1700. For two or three miles Smudger and I walked ahead of the convoy, and felt the better for it. We saw many remains: mules and men, stores, mud, chains, and upturned trucks. Riding was a bumpy business as the trucks jolted from pothole to pothole. If you sat with the driver you clung with both hands to a bar that ran across the dashboard; if you were in the back lying on the baggage you were jerked all the time up and down and from side to side.

In pouring rain we arrived at a clearing near the Manipur River crossing. When summoned we started the engines and brought the trucks down to the river bank, but a queue of vehicles waiting their turn to get on the ferry held us up and we were ordered back to the clearing. After considerable manoeuvring and turning of lorries in mud and rain, we tumbled at nightfall into the backs of the trucks, ate what food we could find in semi-darkness and went to sleep. At 0400 we were roused and woke the drivers. I drove my lorry down myself.

The river was 110 yards wide at the ferry and engineers had rigged a 3 inch steel cable from bank to bank. A large block ran on the cable and to it were fixed wire ropes that held a raft made of wooden planks on steel pontoons. The raft was big enough to take two trucks at a time. Progress over the river was partly by hauling from the far bank but also by slewing the raft as it lay across the current in such a way that the current was used to push it to the far side.

We found the advance party of 7 IMFTU camped on the far bank where the road began to climb a long hill, and in the afternoon I went back over the ferry on foot for news of some of our trucks which had not arrived. They were delayed by a lorry in front of them which, while driving onto the raft, had jolted a truck already there and bumped it forward until its front end overhung the water. The engineers pulled it back and lashed it into place. As I returned I saw from the raft that the body of a dead elephant carried down by the current had stuck on some rocks in midstream. The current there was very swift and strong, and above and below the crossing there were fierce rapids.

Listening to the radio next morning we heard, "This is London calling in the Eastern Service and General Forces Programme of the BBC. Here is the news: Troops of the 5th Indian Division continuing their advance along the Tee-dim Road (they always pronounced Tiddim, Tee-dim) have reached a point on the south bank of the Manipur River." Bill Gleed, outside the tent and trying to shave in a mirror hanging from a sapling, continued the commentary: "This point is fly-ridden. I'm sorry I'll read that again. Here is the latest communique from SEAC Headquarters. Cor, Charles, these flies are bloody awful. You have to keep running-on-the-spot out here all the bleeding time." He was stripped to the waist and his big white belly jerked up and down as he leapt and danced in front of the mirror. The site had been used by a mule transport company before we came and the flies were as bad as I had seen anywhere. We were there a week.

I went for a walk the first afternoon and noticed many skeletons. High up overlooking the river was a machine-gun post manned by a section of Jat sepoys under a British lieutenant. He gave me a mug of their sweet milky tea and we sat on the edge of a trench, looking at his map. The valley at our feet was 2,000 ft below, and his post was at 4,000 ft, not far from a DZ, or supply dropping point. I followed a mule track for about 500 feet to a narrow ridge where there were a few pine trees, short, stunted hardwoods and coarse grass not more than a foot high. I met Chin villagers, stocky men with muscular calves, and children carrying enormous loads. They had been scavenging at the Dropping Zone for bits of rope, tins, parachute material and any cigarettes the NCO in charge might give them for helping to move heavy boxes. A hawk circled around and I saw flocks of small birds with bright red bodies and black heads flying from tree to tree – scarlet minivets. Below the top of the hill was an abandoned Jap camp with all the squalor of defeat – stained dressings in wicker baskets, eating utensils, bits of clothing and everywhere the gnawed remnants of corncobs.

QMS Vedmore, with whom Bill and I had spent hours playing cards at mile 80.5, looked in at the camp on his way home on repatriation; he was extremely talkative and became more so every minute as we plied him with drink to celebrate his good fortune: he had been six or seven years in the Far East. We were a convivial party and Kurup, who had not been able to get out of earshot, said next morning, "Oh what is it all, my Gawd; last night I was suffocated by the swearing language."

Terry and I took a 15-cwt Dodge truck to the DZ at mile 138, where during a drop one had to be alert to escape the fate of an Indian soldier who saw a sack of rice on its way down ('free drop') and ran to take it in his arms. We collected mail for the unit, and the rum ration. With our other rations were cases of tinned 'self-heating soup' for the whole division. As the soup was Oxtail and many of the troops were Hindu, the tins came in the end to units like 7 IMFTU where they were a treat for the British. In each tin was a chemical heater which was lit by putting a match to a wick; a few minutes later the soup was ready and scalding hot, the very thing for troops who were wet and cold and must not light fires.

Here I met the American Field Service (AFS) for the first time. "Hi! I'm Danny James, AFS. Guess I'll be bringing you some sick."

He showed me how to drive his jeep-ambulance: I was delighted with this extraordinary toy – forwards, backwards, two-wheel, four-wheel, high ratio, low ratio; there was nowhere I did not think I could go. Danny came to supper and told me about the AFS. He was a big man, open in manner, modest and unassuming, kind and unselfish. He had had a varied life. He came originally from California but had lived also in New England. He had been to sea as an 'oiler' or stoker on convoys to Murmansk and had been torpedoed. He was paid 60 rupees a month (about £5 in those days). The AFS men's only luxury was access to the American PX, a superior version of our NAAFI canteens, but there was no PX on the Tiddim Road. The AFS men were for one reason or another not fit enough to be in the American Services. Of those I knew one had asthma, another (Danny) had had polio, another had broken legs that had not been properly set, and so on. Without exception they were the sort of men who would go anywhere and do anything if it helped. The ones I got to know drove jeep ambulances fitted with frames to carry stretchers. They seemed indifferent to enemy fire and would put their jeeps at the steepest and roughest ground. They made a major contribution to the survival of our sick and wounded and I was to see more of them later.

From the Manipur River the 5th Indian Division fought its way past Tiddim, Kennedy Peak and Fort White to Kalemyo in the Burma plain, and there joined up with the 11th East Africa Division which had come down the Kabaw Valley. We were supplied entirely by air, and in mountain terrain too steep for landing everything came either by free drop or by parachute, and at first nothing could be flown to India – no mail, for example, and no casualties. These had to wait for evacuation until we reached a place where we could level a strip for a light plane to land, a plane able to take a stretcher and a couple of sitting patients. The job of dropping supplies in those mountains went on through the monsoon and was done by Dakotas of the Royal Air Force. Many years later I came by accident to know some of the pilots and navigators of those aeroplanes and we were able to compare notes about the dropping zones we had both known, they from the air and I from the ground.

When we moved on from milestone 126 the road was dry and the going good. I left with a section that was to open for patients at milestone 144. I should have Bill Gleed, Kurup and several NCOs with me. 7 IMFTU's lorries had been sent back to Imphal, and we were taken forward by a Motor Transport Company allotted to us for the move. The MTCs used 15-cwt 4-wheel-drive Dodge trucks. The drivers were all Pathans from the North West frontier – fine looking men with hook noses, shiny black hair and striking blue eyes. South of Imphal the main rivers and mountain ridges ran north and south; the road ran along the hillsides except where, at intervals, it climbed to cross from one valley to another. By midday we had reached milestone 138 and the convoy halted on a high ridge. To the west the ground fell precipitously; the slope facing us was about 3,000 feet from top to bottom and covered with jungle except where a rare clearing showed the presence of a village. Immediately below me lay the wreck of a Jap tank and I wondered that they had driven tanks along this road. Japanese remains lay in abandoned bunkers and I had to admire what they had accomplished in the face of so much privation.

From farther on, near two more wrecked Jap tanks, I could see south to Tiddim; distant outlines looked bare but all the near hills were jungle-covered save where the Chins had cleared small patches to grow rice and maize. Driving along that road gave me a feeling remembered from the Alps: the drop below, 'sticky' bits that one is glad to have passed, a feeling of no let-up. The wheels had to keep turning and turning so that you did not lose any of the hard-won ground.

When the convoy stopped for a long halt the drivers gathered by my truck, and I tried to talk with them in Urdu. They said that their country (Waziristan) was very like the Chin hills except that there was not so much vegetation. When at home the driver of my truck worked on his farm or at mending roads. In addition to the Lee Enfield that was part of the truck's equipment, he carried a Sten gun and, seeing my interest, he gave me a practical lesson on how to use it. He was, he said, a *Mahsud* and his name was Gulam Kader. He was very proud of his own country where he had six wives and was 'able to rest'. He had joined the army to get better food and clothing. He offered me a chew of tobacco and asked me if my home was Japan. I found his tobacco hot but without flavour; it made the saliva flow.

We reached mile 144 at 1330, and when the rest of the section turned up we pitched camp. The road here was in a deep valley, and once more close to the Manipur River; the view was enclosed except back to the north where we could see a conspicuous mountain with a double summit. By the camp a clear stream with pools and waterfalls came tumbling out of the jungle, and to rise for a cold sponge in that stream contrasted gratefully with waking at Dimapur, sweaty and tired, to bathe in a basin of warm water.

On the first day I walked back to the dropping zone at mile 142 for some of the thickly padded cushions used in parachute drops to break the fall of containers whose contents were fragile. They made comfortable garden seats in camp. The road to the DZ followed the usual steep sort of hillside. Across the valley I could see huts and patches of what looked like standing corn; the scene was enticing but the Manipur River there was full and violent, and ran down fierce rapids; there was not even a bamboo rope bridge and it was hopeless to think of crossing.

When we were at Dimapur we had been visited by the CO of an infantry battalion; he came to see if any of his men were patients at 7 IMFTU; Donald Gunn, who had come out with me on the *Ranchi*, was with him as Regimental MO and I had told John Wakeford afterwards how much a part of me wished I were doing that sort of job. It was natural to want to be more dramatically mixed up in what was going on than we were. At mile 144 we could hear the guns and had been told that a battalion of Dogras was even then attacking Tiddim. Bill, at 43, was like an old war horse; he had found a Jap rifle and some ammunition, and now he got them out for us to do more target shooting. However much he derided the army, he was at heart still a sergeant major in the Gloucesters longing to be more active. Two officers from the West Yorks called one evening to ask if we were satisfied with the arrangements for our defence. It had not occurred to us that there was anything to defend us against and we had no complaint that we knew of, but Bill said, "Defence, eh? Things are looking up, Charles."

We felled trees to make space for the big tents, but until patients began to come in there was little to do. Someone brought a bag of mail from the DZ and news that another bag had been lost. I personally did well by the mail drops; letters and books came regularly and from the time we left India few parcels went astray. In the evenings we got out a gramophone ('welfare') from Sergeant Smith's stores. Smudger had records of all sorts of things, including *Agnus Dei* and *Ave Maria*. We sat under trees in the open and one by one he produced his favourites: "I like this song, Sir; Jeegly and some orchestra it is, conducted by Winkler or some fucker." It was a beautiful aria and when I stole a look at him I saw tears in his eyes.

With a barrel and some planks we made a table which served, with our makeshift garden seat, as an open-air Mess. We entertained two sergeants from a Field Ambulance and played Pontoon with them by the light of a pressure lamp. Bill and I had a suspicion that some officers regarded us as not quite 'pukka' – 'fraternizing with the men' and all that. But I had no doubts about my relationship with the men. If, to be an officer, you had to stand on privilege you had no business to be there.

On 13 October I painted '7 IMFTU' on a signpost and stuck it by the roadside. That afternoon we were in business and began to take in patients. They were brought in day and night and we pumped everyone from up the road for news of the battle for Tiddim. There was nothing much to hear. On 15 October the CO appeared, accompanied by the division's Assistant Director Medical Services (ADMS), a full colonel; they said that progress farther up the road was slow and we must be ready to take up to 200 patients. Bill and I sat outside that evening with Staff Sergeant Edwards and Smudger. I had seen a lot of patients during the day and was glad to sit down. Kurup as usual was in his tent.

I was beginning to be a bit disenchanted with Kurup; his constant and weary "Oh, my Gawd" was getting on my nerves and his helplessness irritated me. When shaving, for instance, he stood before the mirror with his hand out waiting for his batman to put his razor in it, and at table he waited for the batman to rinse his mug and bring it from his tent to his hand. We had been too much together. I took too much notice of his shy Indian prudishness and the little knickers never discarded. Bill believed that if he were abandoned on the road he would "just bloody well sit down and wait for starvation to reach him".

October the sixteenth was the festival of Dewali when Indians hang up lights to celebrate the end of the monsoon and worship Lakshmi, goddess of the earth and of wealth. By a fluke the divisional engineers had wired us that day for electric light from a generator somewhere back along the road and so, as well as the lights from hurricane lamps hanging in trees, we now had the blaze of electric bulbs. Nammu Singh asked me if Division would tomorrow be taking down the bulbs and removing the wires and I had to explain that XIVth Army had not brought us electric light solely for Dewali. We were given a party that night at the Indian lines after which the IORs then came to our Mess with singers and a dancer, a boss-eyed sweeper; he danced to a drummer who used an empty tin for a drum. I hated it because no one took any notice of them and they were doing their best.

Conditions were primitive in the 'wards'. Many of the patients needed saline by intravenous drip, and we sterilized the syringes and other equipment by boiling over an open fire or Primus stove. The actual setting up of drips was often at night; it meant first kneeling in mud at the side of the stretcher while you tried to get a hurricane lamp to shine enough light on the spot where you were trying to put a needle exactly in a vein. The nursing staff of IOR orderlies was wretchedly inadequate and mostly inefficient. Things would have been better if we could have bathed the patients, cooled them, cleaned their mouths and made them drink. On 18 October an Indian soldier was carried in vomiting and so very ill that I immediately took a specimen of blood to look for parasites; I told the stretcher bearers meanwhile to go to the ward with him. Half an hour later when I went there I found that they had thoughtlessly dumped him fully clothed face down on the ground between two stretchers: callous and stupid was what I thought them, as well as bone idle. The crowded conditions in the IOR wards and the stench from unwashed dehydrated bodies and dirty clothing were pretty grim. The BORs fared rather better, with Smudger and a couple of NCOs to run their ward.

We took in many cases of scrub typhus at this time and for many of them we could do little; their moans did not mean pain but that they were very ill. They had sores and ulcers round their mouths, which were dry and dirty; their cheeks were hollow and their lips blue. They had a blotchy, purplish rash, and all the time I heard, "*Bahut kamzori, Sahib, bahut taklif*" – much weakness, much trouble.

On 20 October we were lent a Nursing Sister who came up early and stayed late and did a tremendous amount to transform the look of the place. I wish I remembered her name and whether she was pretty, and whether we talked at all; but no, all I noticed was that when she came the place looked like a slum, and when she went it had almost begun to look like a corner of a hospital ward. That night, after she had gone, one IOR died of typhus and a BOR on my own staff was taken ill with severe abdominal pain.

We were coping now as best we could with large numbers of Indian patients – what a poor lot they seemed! They started moaning and groaning as soon as one came in sight. Some were genuinely very ill and suffered greatly under these conditions, but many were just unwilling to return to duty or to admit that they were a little better. The Dogras and Gurkhas made the best patients, I thought, then the Jats; the rest not so good. I began to sleep badly, thinking about the cases we had in. On the 22nd I meant to take half a day off, but in fact I was too busy seeing a lot of new cases and setting up intravenous drips. A picture of doing the same thing in the sophisticated surroundings of a modern hospital, helped by a neat and efficient sister, came to mind, and now I was doing it in a tent by the light of a hurricane lamp, helped by a half-taught sepoy. Kurup seemed quite incapable when confronted by such things and so I was putting up the drips on his patients as well. He worried dreadfully and would not take any responsibility, least of all for British patients.

A few days later I had two BORs who were very ill indeed; both were deaf and looked blue. One drank fourteen pints of water during the night, and the other, I thought, was going to die. When I knelt by him and asked how he felt (a meaningless question – I just wanted to be company for him) he said, "Not too fucking grand, Sir". I could have cried if I hadn't been to Shrewsbury. Next night another BOR was brought in with a note to say he had collapsed; he was jaundiced and had pain in the abdomen and I decided to keep him under observation. I felt bad myself most of the day; the weather lately had been exhaustingly hot.

The next afternoon a Hindu died and I watched the IORs burn him. They used a tremendous amount of wood, several tins of kerosene and *ghi* (clarified butter) and five gallons of petrol. One of them ran to the pyre and lit a match, nearly cremating himself in the whoof with which the petrol went up. They made a great jolly of the whole thing and it seemed a good party. When it was over the remains were flung down the hillside in hopes that some bits would reach the Manipur River, which flows eventually into the Irrawaddy. I wondered if they thought it flowed into the Ganges. Perhaps it did not matter.

In the evening one of my BORs died. I thought the others might recover if left alone, but I feared that to take them several thousand feet up to Tiddim (which by then had been captured) might be fatal. Smudger called me in the night to attend to a transfusion that was not working; it was a clear cool night with shooting stars, and a crescent moon setting on the edge of a hill. Smudger helped me and we sat out afterwards in the small hours, eating bread and cheese, and drinking mugs of tea.

On 25 October the padre of the Royal West Kents, a good man, came down, and just before lunch we buried a soldier who had died the previous day. It was a simple and moving ceremony: the figures at the grave, the noise of the torrent below, bright sun, blue cloudless sky, the dark greenery of jungle-clad hills all around and the quiet voice of the padre speaking of everlasting life, of dust to dust, and of salvation through Christ. It was more dignified than the Indians' ceremony of the day before when they all rushed round with petrol drums and tins of cooking oil. I did not believe any of it, but the old familiar words gave comfort.

During the last days of October the main part of the unit leap-frogged us and went on to open on the far side of Tiddim. Work was slack again and we renewed our acquaintance with the engineers' Field Park Company five miles away, near a bridge they had built over a tributary stream called the Beltang Lui. We made a habit of walking up to their place in the evenings, winding in and out of side valleys, up and up until we were hundreds of feet above the Manipur River. The moon was half full in a clear starry sky; the valley with steep black hills in shadow on either side and the silvery stream far below was beautiful. We pounded along in gym shoes with our coats open, the brown of our skins showing darker in moonlight than the faded green of our trousers. Ronnie Fulton, the lieutenant in charge of the Field Park Company, was a slim, dark, vital Scot, a collector of Japanese flags and the owner of a black Wiltshire terrier called Scruff. Ronnie usually brought us back to our camp at reckless pace by jeep and we sat there in deck chairs until after midnight, talking about careers, about medicine and engineering.

Soon my section moved on to join the rest of 7 IMFTU on the far side of Tiddim. Tents and gear were loaded on the trucks of a Transport Company at dawn and the convoy moved at 0800. The going was straightforward for the first five miles to the Beltang Lui which we crossed by a small Bailey bridge; then the road began to climb The Chocolate Staircase, a *tour de force* of road-building that went up 3,000 ft in seven miles of zig-zag.

There were fourteen hairpin bends in the first two miles and the whole track up to just under 5,000 ft was carved out of a clayey soil the colour of milk chocolate; at the worst parts tarpaulins, as on The Ladder, were draped on the slope below the road to lessen the likelihood of slips. The 4-wheel-drive trucks went in low gears, wheels turning faster than the trucks advanced up the slope. After the thirtieth hairpin at mile 157 the slope eased where we reached the crest of a narrow ridge at 5,000 ft. East of us the ground dropped to the tangle of valleys and ridges from which the waters of the Beltang Lui flowed. To the west a thickly wooded slope fell to the Manipur 3,500 ft below and only three miles away. Tiddim was five miles on and only 700 ft higher. The road became less steep and after passing through Tiddim village we reached our camp at 6,000 ft. We were among pines and I lay on my back in the sun with my eyes closed, smelling the pines, hearing the wind in the branches, tasting the joy of being on a high place.

Life on the road had been made up of mud and dust, of long halts between movement, of mule trains, tanks, ambulances, convoys of trucks like our own and jeeps on all kinds of business. The white crosses and the Jap skulls perched on sticks were as much a part of the scene as the roadmenders and the statuesque Nagas and Chins; they were as familiar as the dropping zones with their discarded baskets and parachutes, as the burst sacks of flour and the supply planes droning overhead. There were cooking fires, piles of chapattis and the smells of curry; there was everywhere a feeling of pressing on, of being 'in it'. There was a great tendency to decorate and to pick up trophies – flags, kukris, Jap weapons. As we went along we met men of every race and religion – Pathans, Nepalese, Sikhs, Punjabis, South Indians. I remembered how, as we climbed the long dry spur of a hill in convoy one day, we met a jeep bouncing and sliding down in the opposite direction: British officers and their servants going on leave or repatriation. The jeep was piled high with Jap flags, rifles, revolvers, swords, and the young officers with blond

moustaches were gaily dressed – a medal ribbon or two, colourful scarves, jaunty hats and suede shoes with crepe soles. I could
see them still and remembered how dull and pedestrian we had
felt.

Chapter 7

Tiddim

THAT FIRST EVENING at Tiddim I found pale blue orchids growing in a fork of a pine tree. The air was cool and invigorating, the scene breathtaking. The sun set behind dark hills covered by long pale clouds above which the sky was clear. I slept with one blanket over me and it was nothing like enough. I got up at dawn to stand on the edge of a bomb crater and look out over the valleys to the east at far ridges catching the sun; I could hear a very faint distant cockcrow.

In the afternoon I walked a short way back down the ridge to the remains of a bungalow; there was a lawn, a rose border, juniper, geraniums and chrysanthemums, and a white gate that led nowhere. Corporal Odell, the big man who did building jobs for us, had come with me; he was doing some plumbing in camp and was looking for bits of iron pipe and perhaps a tap or two. When we got back to camp the chill of late afternoon, a slight mistiness, the grey light and the tang of smoke from a wood fire reminded me of autumns at home.

As we looked east from camp we saw the summit ridge of Kennedy Peak, 8,871 ft, running roughly north to south across our front. From camp the road climbed on for twelve miles to the left, or north, end of that ridge and disappeared from view at a place called Vital Corner. The road there turned sharply right to run south for a few miles on the far side of Kennedy Peak. The Japs had not yet been dislodged from Vital Corner or Kennedy Peak and as usual they were very well dug in. We watched day after day as our aeroplanes bombed their positions on the ridge. The Hurribombers roared over us and seconds later the whole skyline at which we were looking erupted in flame and smoke. There was a stiff battle for Vital Corner but the escape of the Japanese to the south-east was soon threatened by encircling columns which had already reached the road farther on, near Fort White. On 3 November the last Japs left Kennedy Peak and by the 4th our troops had taken their place.

On the very crest of the ridge at Tiddim, 6,000 feet up, was an old bunker, an unroofed hole about three feet deep and big enough for my camp bed, my tin trunk and a steel ammunition box in which I kept books. To keep me warm I roofed the bunker with a tarpaulin and the QM christened it Plynlimmon Palace. The Manipur River lay at the front door, 4,500 feet below; across the valley was a range of hills 6,000 to 8,000 feet high, labelled on our maps 'fairly dense mixed jungle'. In places I could see clearings and villages. Only one of the hills had a name, Hlang Tang Mual, and was by no means the highest. Immediately below my bunker Sadheo had cut an earth ledge where he lit the fire to heat water in tin cans for my early morning tea and my evening bath which I took in the open where I could watch the sun set over the western mountains. Some yards away along the ridge was the Mess, a tent in which was a 'Sigri', a heater made of a 40-gallon oil drum round the bottom of which we punched holes. In the evening we lit a fire in the drum to burn fircones which were plentiful on the ground. The glowing fire gave out a great deal of heat; we had drinks and meals there and sat round it when our own tents were cold.

The Chins came often to look for treasures like empty tins, food and cigarettes. They had a slinking springy gait which made nothing of the slopes below camp; they smoked pipes and wore their hair long, almost to the shoulder. The men wore a garment like a skirt which ended halfway down the thigh. On their backs they carried bamboo baskets held by the usual headstraps. One old man came up the hill below camp to beg rice. He moved steadily and without a sound. He spoke a little Urdu and we were able to converse in a simple way. I had an idea of coming here on leave one day to camp and roam about the villages, living off the country, but he made it clear that I should have difficulty in finding food. He carried a beautifully polished goblet, the size of a Jaffa orange, made of red-brown wood like mahogany; I took it to be some kind of hookah; there was water inside and it stank of stale tobacco.

The work at Tiddim was light compared with that during the monsoon at Dimapur and back along the Tiddim road. Although the patients were often very sick they were few in number and the wards were never full. We had brought some patients with us from mile 144; they were not yet well enough to return to their units and at that time we had no means of evacuating them to a base hospital. A few new patients with either malaria or typhus began to come in; some of them were unconscious or dehydrated and had to be fed intravenously. Wallace Parke and I between us looked after the BORs, and Terry and the Indian doctors looked after the IORs. Every few days I acted as Orderly MO, almost a non-job except one morning when we had a surprise visit from the Deputy Director of Medical Services, 33 Corps, the same Brigadier Crosbie who had visited us at Dimapur. In our small world the DDMS was a bit of a swell and according to my diary I thought him 'a decent old chap' (he must have been all of 45). Bill Gleed said afterwards, "Charles wore a hat for the Brigadier: the Army Commander would probably rate a shirt as well."

Crosbie brought with him a Lieutenant-Colonel who was just out from home and talked a lot about large scale evacuation of casualties from France by air. I wondered if he knew that Ronnie Fulton was just then trying to level a landing strip for an L.5 in the jungle near Saizang, almost 3,000 feet below us.

On 7 November I walked down the road through Tiddim to our waterpoint from which water was brought to the IMFTU by water cart. All that was left of the village was two brick houses and a collection of about thirty shacks. All had been smashed to a greater or lesser extent and the Chins I found sitting there seemed to be deliberating about rebuilding. There was an abundance of flowers – violet and red convolvulus, pink and white roses, bougainvillea and a great deal of mint in flower. At the waterpoint I found some Indian engineers. I had become curious about hemp and hemp-smoking and as grasses grew thick about the waterpoint I asked the Indians if they could show me hemp growing wild. There were a lot of grins and sly remarks about my only wanting to smoke some myself but they found some for me.

When the new landing strip was finished I went there with a patient in a jeep ambulance; it was a lovely drive along a track that only a jeep could have used. The little aeroplanes used for flying out patients were called L.5s, and took one stretcher and two sitting cases. It was our only way of sending serious cases to hospital. We feared that some convalescents from typhus may have died as a result of flying out like this: typhus affected the heart and for some patients the strain of being flown over mountains at 10,000 feet may have been too much. Ronnie Fulton was in charge at the airstrip and gave me a lift back. He pointed to another village so high and remote that he called it Shangri La: it was Vangte, where Franklyn of 'V' Force had operated a radio transmitter throughout the Japanese occupation. On the way back we stopped to greet a striking looking Chin on whose head, Ronnie said, the Japs had set a great price during the occupation.

On another day I walked 2,000 feet down to a village called Lamzang, following a steep cliffside path. On the way down I found lavender and an aromatic herb called artemisia, with leaves like chrysanthemum. Lower down on a little knoll above the village I passed wooden posts bearing carvings of elephant, deer, rhino, leopard and pig. The Chins told me they marked the site of a grave-yard. The voices of women and children floated up to me, and the low-toned sound of cowbells, reminded me of Switzerland. The village had looked attractive from a distance but when I reached it I was disappointed. The single grassy street had bashas of bamboo and grass on either side; everything was on a slant, and the bashas were held up by stilts on the lower side of the slope. All around were banana trees and stacked corncobs. The bashas were dark and bare inside and the plots where they stood were surrounded by wooden palisades; outside, on posts, were the skulls of deer and of mithun, a buffalo or bison peculiar to this part of the world.

When I sat down to sketch the face of a little boy a crowd of children gathered. Handing the sketch to the sitter I asked him in Urdu, "Is it all right?" He grinned and very shyly whispered, "Thik" – All right. As I was watching a basket-maker in Lamzang some aeroplanes flew overhead and started a hubbub of talk, some of which was directed towards me. After listening for some time I made out an often-repeated phrase that sounded a bit like "Fighter escort" and I noticed that the hut walls were covered with drawings of twin-engined supply planes and fighter bombers.

The birds at Tiddim were easier to see than those in the thick jungle lower down. I had no book about Indian birds with me until later, when I acquired two that were excellent: Salim Ali's *Birds of the Indian Hills* and Whistler's *Popular Handbook of Indian Birds*. My binoculars froze at night when there was cloud and in the mornings it was always a little while before they warmed up and I could focus them. I wrote down descriptions of the birds' colouring and sometimes made sketches from which I was able later to identify jays, nuthatches, scarlet minivet cocks and their orange coloured hens, woodpeckers, a hoopoe, and a black and white bird like a magpie with a red bill; it had a call like iron screeching against iron and was probably a tree-pie. In a wooded ravine I tracked down an elusive bird with a very sweet song, the 'Whistling Schoolboy', not unlike our blackbird in appearance.

Ronnie had moved his company from the Beltang Lui to a place that went towards Vital Corner and at night Smudger and I often walked the three miles to see him. At Ronnie's we did not always only feast and drink and play cards; he liked to fantasize about his past. He was about my age, very dark and lean. He claimed he had a brilliant brain, but that he had been obliged to leave Cambridge after breaking his tutor's jaw in a fight; I never found out why he fought his tutor. He also said he had, or was it had almost had, a blue for boxing. One night he showed me a very large photograph of a most lovely girl and said, after reverently putting it away, "That's what I'm fighting for." I reflected that I had no such romantic reason for being where I was and wondered what reason I would have given if asked – some instinct perhaps for preserving the kind of order in which I had been brought up.

Ronnie was always ready with news from up the road and Bill and I liked to question him; he would expound freely on defensive positions and other military matters. His superiors were with him one night, a lieutenant-colonel and two majors, all thoroughly drunk. One of them had cousins in the ICS for whom he did not have a good word – 'fuckpigs' was the most friendly – 'benevolent, benign, blue-nosed f-pigs'. A heated argument developed between them about the merits of Jat Sikhs and Musbi Sikhs, whatever they might be, but cooled when we were served an enormous meal. The conversation moved from the wickedness of their cousins to the merits of a scheme by which the engineers encouraged Chins to kill Japs by making poles for them on which to stick the heads of any Japs they caught.

On another night Ronnie invited me to join him on a trip down to mile 150 to pick up some hose pipes. He had a very good and intelligent NCO with him, a Naik who was always known as '51', the last two digits of his army number. '51' sat in the back with Scruff, Ronnie's Wiltshire terrier, in his arms. Everywhere was deserted and quiet after the passage of the division. Our destination was a waterpoint by a wrecked Japanese tank, and on the way Ronnie stopped at the grave of a friend, a Lieutenant RE, called Lane, who had driven his jeep over one of the 17th Division's mines which had been dug up and replanted by the Japanese.

When Smudger and I went up to Ronnie's on our last evening at Tiddim we found him in bed with malaria; I dosed him and we enjoyed a quieter evening together than was usual in his restless company.

At dawn I heard once more the long drawn out crow of cockerels, the sounds floating across the valleys from villages far below. I did not look forward to the prospect of going down to the heat of the Burma plain.

Terry and I left Tiddim in convoy on 14 November. The track wound along a crest, sometimes in sun, sometimes in shadow, to Vital Corner. On the right we looked down to the Saizang airstrip and up to Kennedy Peak and on the left we looked back to Tiddim and down the Chocolate Staircase. After Vital Corner the track followed a hillside covered with dense jungle like that at Dimapur: big trees, luxuriant creepers. In places the trees were broken, stripped of foliage and uprooted, and the ground was scarred with bomb craters and the remains of strongpoints and dugouts. Near the summit of Kennedy Peak the jungle was so devastated that there was very little to obstruct the view south-east to the lower hills, to Fort White and Burma. The valleys were filled with billowing cloud, brilliantly white against the empty blue sky. Sitting in front with the driver was like being on some high-level scenic tour of Switzerland without the snow. At Fort White we turned off right along the track to look for a camp site. Below camp there was dank jungle with mosses and ferns where in the first half-hour I found five different kinds of orchid in flower growing on stumpy trees within fifty yards of my tent. Above us were bare grassy hills, gently curved but steep. We thought that the camp, at about 7,500 feet, was likely to be our highest, so we raided the medical comforts for a bottle of champagne to celebrate.

The night was cold and I was up before dawn. I climbed a grassy knoll to get warm and came on a platoon of Dogras just getting out of their bivouacs. There was a thin layer of frost on the ground and they shivered with cold. The main range stretched north and south. To the west was the big depression of the Manipur River and beyond were more peaks rising to 8,000 feet and over. To the north Kennedy Peak showed clear where the road cut across it. To the east the country fell away.

The plain was covered by low dense white cloud through which two lesser ranges emerged like long reefs from the sea; they ran north and south. The sky above the horizon was full of changing colour. Then, in a nick of the farthest hills, an arc of the sun suddenly showed, red and bright and growing in size as I watched. I had a feeling of the earth's turning, of this immense blue and rosy plain with its mists and rivers, its jungles and paddy fields, moving with unbelievable speed towards the sun. Then the light flooded the hill on which I stood. Curling spirals of smoke rose among the trees where the Dogras were lighting fires. I came down warm and happy to find a mug of tea in the tent and Sadheo shivering over it and wringing his hands with cold.

I spent the rest of the day sketching the various orchids I had found and talking to John Wakeford who was going down to recce a campsite south of Kalemyo. As it seemed likely we were coming to the end of our time together I reminded him of my wish to be posted to a regimental job.

After seeing the CO off to Kalemyo, Terry, Kurup and I set off to climb a ridge of one of the local hills. Terry was soon a long way ahead and long before we reached the ridge Kurup sank to his knees, lay down and said that he could not see. He had only fainted so I sat down and sketched until he felt well enough to make his way to the shade of a tree. He had been convinced, he said, that he was going to die.

On 18 November we woke early, expecting the General Purpose Transport Company (GPT). A bank of cloud filled the valley but above it the sky was clear and The Plough and Arcturus showed. I lit a roaring blaze in the mess tent and we washed and shaved in luxury. 1000 hours and still no trucks. At 1430 Bill Gleed and I walked back to the fork where the Falam track left the track down to Kalemyo and learnt that our trucks were held up at Fort White; we walked there and whiled away the afternoon shivering and smoking until the GPT officer invited us into his tent for a toddy. He was a Scot and talked to us about his Pathans, of whom he was very proud.

We did not leave until 1830. It was already dark. After a slow and bumpy journey with many twists and turns, always downhill, and after many pauses and waits we reached our destination. Eight miles down the road at Stockade 2, about 1,000 feet above sea-level, we could see light and, rounding one more corner, came suddenly on a big camp fire. The light of the flames flickered on the brown faces and bare arms of a group of BORs, lighting up the tall straight trunks of teak and, to our surprise, the steel nose and gun muzzle of their tank, parked quietly like a docile elephant in the trees behind them.

We came on down through the forest until at Stockade 1 we met troops of the 11th East African Division which had fought its way down the Kabaw Valley; there was silence, and blackout, forms sleeping in slit trenches and silent negro guards with sten guns. A few miles farther on we came to a crossroads – Kalemyo, a white wooden signpost with a single finger pointing back the way we had come – 'Tiddim 48 miles'.

Kalemyo was on the edge of the dry belt of the Burmese plain and away from the great teak forests; our immediate surroundings were flat and low, and although we were not much more above sea-level than we had been at Dimapur the climate in December was pleasant by comparison. We were in open scrub instead of the tangled jungle of Assam and the Chin hills; here and there were clumps of banana palms, and dotted about the camp were termite hills and some small trees with huge broad rough leaves called 'bastard teak'. The days were hot and the nights cold enough for me to wear a serge battledress top after sundown. In the mornings I woke to hear flights of green parakeets screaming overhead, a sound of the plains, and there were pied and green woodpeckers, fantail flycatchers, grey and white bulbuls, pied mynahs and a rufous-backed shrike which regularly perched on our single telephone wire.

A small river, the Zi Chaung, ran down from the hills not far from camp, and the hard earth 'road' near our tents crossed it by a ford where the river was a foot deep and twenty yards wide and clear water ran over brown pebbles. Upstream of the ford some engineers had built a springboard and one could dive and swim in a pool of cold water about seven feet deep. I often met the AFS ambulance drivers there and visited their Mess which was not far away. The AFS headquarters was run by a genial figure called Ed Spavin from New Bedford, Mass.; he had once sailed in the Newport to Bermuda yacht race and his ambition, which I shared for an evening, was to find a sailing boat in the Far East and sail it home. The AFS wore what clothes came to hand and their discipline was free and easy. Danny James, whom I met on the Tiddim road, was one day driving his jeep at speed down the Kabaw Valley; it was the dry season and he raised a great cloud of brown dust behind him; he was overtaken by an angry divisional commander (General Gracey) who stopped him and asked if he did not know that there was a fifteen mile an hour speed limit to keep down dust clouds because they would betray our positions to the enemy. Danny got out of his jeep and smiling tolerantly said, "Why General, you don't win wars at 15 mph."

By the roadside away from camp we began to meet Burmese; they were quite different in appearance from the Chins; they were slender, their faces were finer, and they wore long white or coloured linen skirts called *lungyi*. At their sides hung long knives or *dah*. They moved with an easy gait at the side of the road and smoked fat white cigars made of rolled maize leaf. "If Churchill saw one of those he'd chuck all 'is cigars away and stick to Woodbines," said Corporal Odell, who was observant and inter-

9. Captain Heathcote RAMC
(see p.27).

10. Captain Parke RAMC (see
p.32).

11. Kurup "came from the Malabar coast and had the very black skin of the Dravidian" (p. 36).

12. Major Warren Bugler, "quiet, observant, intelligent and perhaps a bit religious" (p. 152).

Warren Bugler
11/9/4:

13. "I made friends with a young girl called Ma Kyia" (p.153).

14. Maung Hla "was a good sort, glad to be of help" (p.159).

15. Charlie Armour: "red-haired and freckle-faced and looked about 17" (p.163).

16. The author (right), Jesselton, February, 1946.

ested in all he saw. One day he brought me a flat-headed fish which he had found three feet underground in damp mud when digging a trench for a latrine. The little fish had well-developed pectoral fins and tail and was about 2½ inches long; we supposed that it was waiting for the rainy season.

Near us at a place called Htoma Myauk an airstrip was hacked out of the jungle; it was of bare earth and when finished was used to bring us supplies and fly patients out. Before long a Mobile Surgical Unit arrived and soon was joined by a Casualty Clearing Station. There was a big influx of doctors and Nursing Sisters (QAIMNS). They seemed not to belong to our simple way of life. On those nights the moon shone in a clear starry sky, the great trees were motionless and in the elephant grass, dry earth and scattered anthills the silence was broken only by chirping crickets and the distant hum of a lighting plant at the Surgical Unit.

American pilots came to see us near Kalemyo, for Dakotas flew daily between Imphal and Htoma Myauk. These Americans were kitted out with everything the modern jungle fighter needs. They had uniforms with badges, knee-length boots and gaiters, sunglasses, and long-peaked caps; they were armed to the teeth with automatic pistols and jungle knives. The nearest Japanese were not less than 20 miles away and we found it difficult to take our visitors seriously, particularly when we found how indefatigable they were in their search for trophies, Japanese relics, bits of uniform, tin hats, and especially those big white silk flags with the red rising sun in the middle.

On 3 December I had a trip to Imphal. The Dakota had no seats and I sat with some convalescent patients on empty baggage sacks in the body of the plane. I had only flown in a Dakota once before and the sudden roar of the engines and the gathering of enormous speed seemed to be taking us to inevitable doom: the trees on either side flashed by, faster and faster and only yards away; there were no signs of leaving the ground and I thought we must crash into the jungle at the end of the strip, when suddenly and miraculously we were floating above the tree-tops.

We flew at several thousand feet and to the west, above massed white cumulus, saw the tops of the mountains through which we went to Tiddim. The pilot asked me to sit with him and I could then look down on the length of the Kabaw Valley and see the winding road from Tamu to Palel and the battle-scarred hilltops where 20th Indian Division had held the Japanese advance on Imphal a few months earlier.

From the air Imphal seemed big, my first sight of semi-civilization for three months; I had a strong desire for shops, cinemas and restaurants, none of which were to be had. I found the Anglo-Burman corporal who was to travel back with me, and the rations of beer and spirits I was expected to bring. I started back for the airfield with Corporal Riley and on the way passed a squadron of tanks raising clouds of dust as they lumbered in the opposite direction. They bore the names of Scottish mountains – Ben Lawers, Ben Dearg and so on. The Betty 'B', our Dakota of the morning flight, was waiting for us on the airstrip. We flew low and I saw the Kabaw Valley in detail, including the villages of Tamu and Witok. I had a warm welcome at Kalemyo for I had with me some Scotch – 'White Horse'. I could not tell one brand from another, but we all certainly knew the difference between Scotch and Canadian Club rye, the sort of whisky that usually came with the rations. I also brought news that Kalewa, on the Chindwin 15 miles east of Kalemyo, had been taken that day by the East Africans.

Once or twice in early December we had single, heavy downpours of rain, not long lasting, and on the morning of the 10th I woke to find it foggy, dark and cold. The fog cleared quickly after sunrise. That day the Army Commander came unannounced to inspect us. All I wrote in my diary was, "Slim came round this morning – he looked like a brusque farmer, perhaps feeling out of place in a hospital."

When I had seen a bit of India I began to enjoy reading Kipling's books about it. McKeown, the QM, found me one evening over one of them and after a few drinks rather surprisingly denounced Kipling, saying, "Of course, he was the worst kind of imperialist you can get." He added after a pause, "The best thing Kipling ever said was a remark of P.C. Wren's describing a garrison sermon: 'Dearly beloved brethren – and you men there!'"

I took on a new batman, Ram Raj, when I sacked Sadheo. Ram Raj's routine was always the same: I would be at the table reading by the light of a hurricane lamp and would hear him coming. He appeared, shadowy, at the tent door, there was a ringing click of the heels and a not very military salute; I would turn to him, say, "Morning, Ram Raj" and smile. So much notice mildly embarrassed him and he started looking in unlikely places for my mug; when his eye lit on it quite near him, he clutched it with both hands, uttered a 'Huh' of triumph and shambled off to get my tea, crooning to himself. Sometimes his departure was accompanied by nose-clearing noises which I found unpleasant.

Before Christmas I flew to Imphal again to enquire about a jeep which the Unit had been promised. Don put me up and at Base Supply Depot we found a brand new jeep waiting to be collected. We went to the airstrip to see about my flying back that day to Kalemyo as planned, but instead of the American pilots' usual cheery greeting we found an RAF crew. They had taken over from the USAAF since the previous day. They looked coldly at us, told us they gave no lifts, and said that all passages must be booked through XIVth Army HQ. At 'Army', while we waited our turn outside a door marked RAF, another door opened and the Army Commander came down the passage. It was only a week since I had seen Slim at Kalemyo but if I had never seen him I could not have mistaken that face and jaw. We stiffened against the wall and he passed with a kindly enough greeting. 'Army' said that I should have to wait some days to fly back so I decided that instead of flying I would drive the jeep down myself that night.

Until the evening I passed the time in the Imphal bazaar with Smudger, who had come with me for the trip. The Manipuris are very handsome by repute and in the bazaar we had a chance to confirm this. The women had attractive mongoloid features, rounded cheeks and beautiful glossy black hair. Their figures were upright with long straight limbs, rounded but not fat. They wore a kind of sari which left the shoulders bare; I saw none with veils. Their skin was light brown; on their backs they carried chubby little brown babies with straggly black hair, slit eyes and tiny very prominent eyebrows. The atmosphere was like that in every eastern bazaar. No one appeared much interested in business, a customer was rather a nuisance, breaking the thread of talk with cronies or rousing the shopkeeper from a pleasant sleep.

I returned to Don's place at 1700 to pack the jeep with Smudger, a Havildar Chabha, and a sepoy servant of his (it was not unusual for havildars to have sepoy servants). We put in rations, filled up with petrol and fixed up sidescreens and hood: it would be chilly at night. We left in darkness at 1900 after supper and a tot of rum. As far as Palel the road was level and tarred; grasses, hillocks, a cross-wind and the stars reminded me of driving over moorland at home. After Palel the road began to wind up into the mountains and we passed a long convoy coming the other way. I had not driven a jeep at night and was very unpopular with oncoming traffic because I could not find the dip switch; by the time I had found it near my foot the convoy had passed and we were alone. The road, 'as wide as a single bed', turned and twisted up into mist and cold to a pass, then down to a river, then up again to another pass and down to Tamu where we halted at 0100 for a brew. We lit a mixture of petrol and water in a tin can and boiled water for tea. We continued down the Kabaw Valley, fording streams, crossing bridges, losing all sense of direction in mist and dark until at 0400 I decided to call a halt. By then I had become an automaton, my mind far away, but every now and then being brought back to the present by some problem of the road. In the headlights the great jungle trees took on, in my half-sleep, fantastic shapes; often they looked like weird draped old women with raised arms and pointing fingers and seemed to crowd in on either side of us. Sometimes I had the illusion that I was driving between rows of buildings, tall bashas, but there were only trees. Sometimes I thought that Smudger beside me was leaning forward intent on the road; actually he was lying back fast asleep, a blanket over his head. Chabha yawned loudly at intervals in the back and the sepoy was curled up asleep on the floor at his feet.

We occasionally saw spotted, cat-like animals and every now and then a stench reminded me that there were bodies about and that in this apparent solitude of jungle a firearm would be comforting. When we stopped by a stream at 0400 we had come 30 miles from Tamu. We spread our blankets on the shingle; I slept on and off until 0600 when we got up, made more tea, and ate a fried chapatti before going on. Lying out on the shingle, occasionally opening an eye to see if the jeep was still there, I had had a desolate, abandoned feeling. The mist was thick and the gloom and flatness of the surroundings made the Kabaw Valley at night seem very lonely and spooky. After dawn I just sat and drove, dully, choosing the ruts and holes which seemed least objectionable.

After Corps HQ, where we filled up with petrol, the dust began and we were all thickly coated with it when we reached Kalemyo at 1330. We had covered 170 miles in 18½ hours, including a 3-hour halt, an average of 10 mph. I was dirty, dishevelled, unshaven and burning from the sun and the hot dusty air, and needed a bath and a change. The CO was so pleased to have a new vehicle on the establishment that he forgot to be surprised that I could drive, and Mac appointed me chauffeur to the Post Corporal. It was a time when there was no real work to do, and it was nice, I told him, to have a good steady job at last.

On 22 December Mac and I left by jeep at 0700 to do the Unit's Christmas shopping. We had an enjoyable drive with the screen down, the cool air blowing through our clothes, sunlight and cloud shadow on the Chin hills in the west. There was the delight of hurtling past other traffic and the extraordinary pleasure given to the driver by the power of a jeep.

We reached Supply Depot at 0930 but it was 1445 before we got away, what with queues, clerks and overworked Havildars. Laden with December's rations we crawled back, clinking loudly for on top of our rations we had four sacks of beer bottles. We travelled at 5–10 mph, carefully skirting potholes, often waiting for dust to clear after the passage of a truck in the opposite direction. At one spot we stopped to stretch our legs where the Myittha River ran by the roadside. We watched a pied kingfisher flying, hovering, manoeuvring, hovering again and again and then gliding down at an angle with a few wing beats to hit the water with a ringing plop and come out with a fish in its bill.

Early on Christmas Eve we started the celebrations with a sundowner and by Boxing Day everyone was a bit so-so, especially Mac. On 27 December I left to go on leave, Mac coming with me as far as Calcutta.

There was a wide choice of places to go on leave. Some liked the bright lights of the clubs and hotels of Calcutta; others chose to spend their leave at one of the several hill stations where the climate was good and limited social amenities could be found: Ootacamund in the Nilgiri hills, Kashmir where one could live on a houseboat, and Nainital or Darjeeling from which one could look at the highest mountains of the world. Because distances were great and the means of travel crowded and slow it might easily take several days to reach one of the distant leave stations. A sensible system was therefore in use by which, if you had two weeks' leave, the two weeks began after you reached your chosen station and ended when you left it. But for this custom it would have been possible for a man starting on leave from Kalemyo and going to Kashmir, for example, to reach Kashmir on the last day of his leave.

My idea was to go to a hill station near the big mountains and see how close to them I could get. I chose Darjeeling partly because it was nearest to Calcutta and partly because the name had magic associations; it had been the starting point of the early expeditions to Everest and Kanchenjunga and as far as I knew it was the only place outside Nepal where the Sherpa people, of whom I had read a good deal, were to be found. It was next to impossible in Burma in wartime to find at a few days' notice someone to share my idea of leave, so I decided to go alone, carrying my gear, sleeping under a 'Bivvy' tent; in my ignorance I hoped I might get far enough in two weeks to achieve some minor peak. Not having been through any of the 'usual channels' or made any 'contacts' I had to content myself with a ten-day winter trek along the Singalila ridge with a likeable young Sherpa porter.

High and winding, the ridge ran roughly north-west towards Kanchenjunga, 46 miles away. North and east of the ridge was Sikkim, accessible to foreigners only by permission of the Government of India. To the west, on the south side of the Himalayan range, lay the closed and secret kingdom of Nepal, home of the Gurkhas, a land of great mountains including Makalu, Everest, Lhotse and many other peaks as well as the whole of the west side of Kanchenjunga. At that time Nepal was almost totally closed to foreign travellers whose eyes, from the Singalila ridge, could only gaze across the tangle of hills with yearning. Kanchenjunga, knocking one off balance by its height, mass and nearness made other peaks look insignificant by comparison.

Looking back on my leave I seemed to have achieved nothing, but I had seen mountains of a size and splendour that no amount of reading, no photographs, could have made real to me. I had found a closeness that makes relationships with Sherpas easy; I had found that I could live in this country on what I could find in villages by the way and I had learnt something that I could not describe but which I knew would make future expeditions easier.

Chapter 8

Central Burma

BY THE END of December, 1944, XIVth Army had pushed the Japanese out of the mountains and across the Chindwin. East of the Chindwin was a range of low hills, the Zibyu Taungdan, and beyond them a plain that stretched to the Irrawaddy; the small towns of Ye-U, Shwebo and Monywa were in that plain in a loop of the Irrawaddy. Slim had expected the Japanese to make a stand in the Shwebo plain with the Irrawaddy and Mandalay behind them; he had made plans accordingly, expecting a decisive battle in which 33 Corps and 4 Corps would play the chief parts.

However, after crossing the Chindwin in December the Allied advance towards the Irrawaddy was faster than expected and in January, when I reached Comilla on my way back from leave, Ye-U and Shwebo were already in Allied hands. There had been strong rear-guard actions and every town and village had had to be fought for, but it had become clear that the enemy was going to make his main stand east of the Irrawaddy and not with his back to that river.

During December, therefore, Slim made far-reaching alterations to his plans. He decided to attack across the Irrawaddy and towards Mandalay from the north and west as before, but at the same time he would also make a secret thrust south along the Gangaw Valley to *reach Nyaung-U; there he would again cross the Irrawaddy and take Meiktila. Japanese communications with the south would be cut and their forces in Central Burma would be isolated.*

To put the new plan into effect Slim had to alter the dispositions of his troops. He wanted 4 Corps for the secret push to Meiktila, but wished the Japs to believe that they were still opposed at Mandalay by the combined force of 4 Corps and 33 Corps. He therefore left a division of 4 Corps in the north, attaching it for operational purposes to 33 Corps. The rest of 4 Corps made its way to the Gangaw Valley.

When, after my leave, I rejoined 33 Corps (to which 7 IMFTU belonged) most of these regroupings had been carried out and HQ 33 Corps was at Ye-U. 7 IMFTU was still unemployed at Kalemyo but was due any day to move to Sadaung village, south-east of Shwebo. At Shwebo a Casualty Clearing Station was installed.

Some of the details of the changes in 4 Corps and 33 Corps brought about by Slim's regroupings were as follows:

Before the change of plans the main body of troops in the Irrawaddy loop had been 19th Division in the north, 2nd British Division in the centre (opposite Mandalay) and 20th Division at Monywa. Behind them, coming from Imphal, were 7th, 17th and 5th Indian Divisions.

19th and 7th Indian Divisions had hitherto formed 4 Corps, and 2nd British, 20th Indian and 5th Indian Divisions had formed 33 Corps. The change of plan, which Slim hoped completely to hide from the Japs, left 19th Division in the north with 2nd British and 20th Indian Divisions, while 7th and 17th Indian Divisions and a number of other important units silently and secretly made their way south, down the west bank of the Myittha and Irrawaddy Rivers towards Nyaung-U, near Pagan; there they composed the striking force for the attack across country on Meiktila. 5th Indian Division was in Army reserve behind 4 and 33 Corps. Meanwhile the illusion that 4 Corps was still active in the north of the Shwebo plain was maintained by giving the Japs over the radio the busy and complicated but in fact wholly faked wireless traffic of an imaginary 4 Corps.

By mid-January 19th Indian Division in the north, 2nd British Division south-east of Shwebo and 20th Indian Division in the confluence of the Irrawaddy and Chindwin were getting into position facing the Irrawaddy; 7th and 17th Indian Divisions and their accompanying units were on their way south to Myaung-U, and Slim was in the position of which he wrote later in Defeat into Victory:

"The Divisions of the Fourteenth Army were now, in the second week of January, approaching – or, in the case of 19th Division, were actually on – the Irrawaddy along a front of over two hundred miles, from Wuntho in the north to Pakokku in the south. The Japanese, as far as we knew, were still unaware of our change of plan and of the stealthy march of 4 Corps; their eyes, we hoped, were still fixed on Mandalay, not Meiktila. The stage was set for that most dramatic of all military operations – the opposed crossing of a great river."

Slim's strategy was to induce the Japanese to concentrate their strength against the divisions of 33 Corps ranged on the Irrawaddy shore from Wuntho to Myingyan, so leaving Meiktila weakly defended. His greatest single ally was mastery of the air: in the months to come the Japanese could be bombed and the Allies supplied from the air without fear of interference, for in the first half of 1945 there was in Burma no Japanese air attack of any significance.

I had no reason to return by Calcutta and decided to make my way back to Burma by changing at Parvatipur to the metre-gauge Bengal & Assam Railway. It would take me to the Brahmaputra at Amingaon where I could cross by steamer to Gauhati. From Gauhati a train to Dimapur and a hitch with a lorry driver to Imphal and down the Kabaw Valley would get me to Kalemyo, I thought, in three days. It was not to be: it had been easy in December to leave Burma in a half empty aeroplane but in January the road route to Imphal and on to Kalewa was crammed with traffic. Unattached travellers like me were diverted at Gauhati to go by rail to Comilla and be flown to Burma from there. There were many of us and we angrily endured days of delay in transit camps while we fought to get on trains and aeroplanes going our way.

I waited two days at Gauhati for a train, trying with my pencil to catch the feel of the huge river. A group of Anglo-Burmese policemen were there waiting to return to Burma. They told me how they walked out through the Hukaung Valley in the monsoon of 1942, how men and women died on the way, how rafts loaded with refugees too weak to move broke up in the rivers; no one could ever count the dead but the policemen thought they numbered four in every ten. They remembered cold, starvation, exhaustion and disease of every kind, and it puzzled me that what they seemed to have minded most was that they finished the appalling journey barefoot, as if the ultimate indignity for this uniformed force had been to be without boots.

On the night of 21 January I was flown from Comilla to Shwebo. When I went on leave Shwebo had been in Japanese hands, but now it seemed that supply planes bringing reinforcements and men from leave were already landing there. No one knew where 7 IMFTU might be and I was advised to go to 33 corps HQ at Ye-U to ask. At Corps Headquarters the Deputy Assistant Director of Medical Services told me that 7 IMFTU was where I had left it and promised me a lift there in a jeep that evening.

Kalemyo was over 100 miles back and I fell asleep when we were about 15 miles from Kalewa, only waking when we rattled over the famous new Kalewa bridge, the longest Bailey bridge in the world.

The part of Burma between the Chindwin and the Irrawaddy was low and undulating and variously wooded; there was dense jungle in places, open scrub or grass in others. In the dry season, December and January, it was very lovely, green and full of bird life, a paradise.

Within a week, as was the army way, I was travelling through it again by jeep, on my way forward this time with the IMFTU to Sadaung, beyond Shwebo. We were in a long line of traffic driving through cool, wooded gorges with clear streams and sandstone cliffs; in places the road was supported by scaffolding on the faces of cliffs. The dirt track had been made usable for a time by covering its surface with tarred hessian known as *bithess*. Every few miles we stopped for one of those long halts that were usual when moving in convoy on a single track. During one halt at a dusty, hot place where we brewed tea all afternoon, I walked on after dark to discover why we had stopped. It was a place where the track dipped down into a small ravine and turned sharply before climbing the far side of the dip. A laden tank transporter was stuck at the bottom. Floodlights showed the tank, the trunks of jungle trees all round us, and a big recovery vehicle with a crane that had been backed down to hook on the transporter. The floodlit scene was dominated by a squat, powerful figure dressed in dungarees and peaked baseball cap, unmistakably a Japanese, and as unmistakably American. He directed operations with vivid gestures, and in a loud, clear

American voice. The tank and its transporter were hauled out and we moved on.

From Ye-U the track followed the Mu canal where pied kingfishers hovered over the water. The commonest birds were the big vultures: there were flocks of them feeding on bodies by the wayside or farther off, perching and quarrelling in the branches of trees. I stopped for a soldier who was thumbing a lift and when I asked the usual sorts of question I found he was from Bangor in North Wales. We lapsed into Welsh; yes, he was in the Royal Welch Fusiliers (I knew they were in the 2nd British Division, not far away); he was in Animal Transport and looked after mules. Thirty years later we met again when I was living in Bangor and his wife happened by chance to be working for us.

At Sadaung the original 7 IMFTU was together for the last time. On the second night we gave a party for John Wakeford: he was leaving in the morning to take over as CO of a General Hospital. After he had gone Wallace Parke acted as our CO, and when a message came to say that 16 CCS at Shwebo was asking for another MO he sent me. I went reluctantly because I was still hoping to be transferred to a more active sort of life. 16 CCS became very busy when the Battle of the Irrawaddy Shore began, but for the time being there was no work for anyone and I was appointed 'Resuscitation Officer', in charge of a small ward where the worst of the wounded would be treated before operation.

A lot of new officers came in at the same time as me, including a regular IAMC lieutenant-colonel with a monocle. He kept the rum going round, said that every MO should do six years' acclimatization in India before going to the front, and advised abolition of the RAMC. He got on the nerves of some of the junior doctors and 'Stretcher Bearer Officers' who took him seriously. They talked a lot about a Sergeant Pyke who had not come back from leave; he was known to them as Sergeant 'fucking' Pyke because of the monotony of his language. It seemed that he had encountered a newly commissioned officer of the Women's Army Corps (India), on Chowringhi, Calcutta's main street, and had failed to salute. She was Eurasian, very attractive and smartly dressed, but touchy to a degree. When she pulled him up he retorted, "Salute yer, by Christ; you say fuckin' Salaam to me," and was now doing 28 days somewhere in the cooler.

I was delighted to be rescued from this dreary group when Terry came next day with a signal posting me to a fighting formation, the 20th Indian Division.

Chapter 9

*The Myinmu Bridgehead
(111 Anti-Tank Regiment, RA)*

AT DAWN I was climbing into the cockpit of an L.5, the aeroplane
that was to take me to Headquarters 20th Indian Division, 50 miles
away at Monywa on the Chindwin. The plane was of the kind
we used for evacuating the sick and wounded from near
Tiddim. Behind the pilot there was room only for me and my
bedding roll.

The pilot started the engine and we taxied off and rose into the
air in one movement, with no pause; we flew low over the tree-
tops and I could see houses and people, footpaths and cart tracks;
we were low enough for me to pick out the different trees like
mango and banana. I had never flown in a very small aeroplane
and the experience was utterly different from being taken about

as though by bus in a Dakota. It was real flying, like being a bird. Sometimes I felt, "If we don't swoop up now we won't get over that next lot of trees". The country was flat and rather bare except where dark clumps of bamboo and mango marked the sites of villages or tamarinds showed the line of a road. I leaned out of the open cockpit to look down and lost my cap over the side, so that at Monywa I reported to my new colonel, the Assistant Director of Medical Services, hatless, improperly dressed.

Fortunately nobody, least of all Colonel Jackson, took notice of such a trifle, and it only bothered me when I had to return the smart salutes of the Gurkhas who seemed to be everywhere. Monywa was more the size of a large village than a town. The buildings were damaged by shelling but there were enough left for Divisional Headquarters; the place had a brisk and busy air very different from that of the units behind the lines to which I was accustomed. Everywhere on signposts and vehicles I saw the divisional sign – an arm brandishing a curved white sword on a black background.

Colonel Jackson was a big fair-haired Irishman in his late thirties. He was good-humoured and always came straight to the point; I liked him at once. At that time MOs in the Division were either on the strength of a Field Ambulance or were attached by the ADMS to a regiment or battalion. I always felt more directly responsible to Jackson than to the CO of any unit to which I was posted. The crossing of the Irrawaddy by 20th Indian Division under Lieutenant-General Gracey was to start in two days and Colonel Jackson was short of British MOs. He wasted no time: "Get along to 111 Anti-Tank Regiment and tell them you're their new doctor. They're near Allagappa; there's some transport going down to the Field Ambulance there and you can go in that."

The road was busy with jeeps and trucks and on every side I could see the signboards of units belonging to the Division. I got everywhere a deep impression of men quietly putting the last touches to their preparation for battle. After nearly 30 miles I was put down by a signpost painted blue and red for Artillery. I walked along a dusty track between bushes to a group of tents marked RHQ for Regimental Headquarters.

The Regiment had been raised in the West Country as a Territorial Anti-Aircraft Unit: many of the men were from Devon and, except for the CO and one or two others the officers, were civilians who had learnt to be gunners. They were equipped with anti-tank guns and three-inch mortars, and in action they had two roles: sometimes with their anti-tank guns they were expected to hold off enemy tanks, and sometimes their batteries of mortars were on call to give supporting fire to the infantry.

The CO struck me as highly-strung, imperious and nervy, and his frequent smile made me write in a letter "the smiler with the knife under the cloak". He had a reputation for eccentricity based in part on his having laid out a golf course on which to practise firing his 3-inch mortars with live ammunition. He was generally known as 'The Mad Mullah'. For the Irrawaddy crossing the whole of the artillery of 33 Corps was being made available to the Division and the Mad Mullah had been appointed to direct its fire to the far side of the river. His head was so full of the fact that he had been chosen to do this that he had little time to tell me anything except what a lot of firepower would be under his direction: four regiments of 25-pounders, a Medium regiment, self-propelled guns and I forgot what else.

For a week I saw no more of him and in his absence operational control of the Regiment was in the hands of a large, placid major called by everyone 'Jumbo'. He looked like a Jumbo and I felt that here was a man with whom you knew exactly where you were. His language was startling even by BOR standards and on the surface he seemed short-tempered; in fact he was kindly and good-natured and as far as I could judge good at his job. The men liked and respected him. Steve, the Adjutant, a man of say 30, had been a sheep-farmer in New Zealand. He was a Cornishman, tall, big-boned, dark, with high cheek-bones, a long jaw and a deep laughing voice. I liked him in small doses; he was cheery, forceful and quick and never dull. The Quartermaster, Percy, or Captain Percival, was a regular soldier of about 40 who had just been given the MBE. He was taciturn but obliging; at times he seemed lacking in confidence and, until we got to know each other, I found him either a bit aggressive or quietly depressed. In appearance he was of medium height, fair, a bit paunchy, his back straight as a ruler. Ask him for something and you got a brusque, almost rude refusal:

fifteen minutes later and the thing for which you had asked was there. He knew that I had been mostly with Indian troops and he took the trouble tactfully to explain that managing the men from Devon might be different from managing Indians; he may have thought that I just shouted at Indians. He became one of the people I liked best. When I arrived everyone was in a whirl of business except the Padre. I was handed over to him to be shown round and to listen to his complaints of how out of everything he felt.

Regimental Headquarters was on flat ground about two miles from the Irrawaddy among scrubby bush and cactus. The earth was hard-baked and the track which ran by the camp was deep in dust; tarpaulin shelters, guns hidden under camouflage netting, and gun-towing trucks which I learnt later to call 'Quads' were scattered here and there in the dry scrub. The men and NCOs worked stripped to the waist, Warrant Officers wearing their badges of rank on cloth bands round their wrists. The imminence of action, the way in which every man seemed to be getting ready for a job he knew, made me glad to be one of them. The Shwebo I had left only that morning seemed far away and as much a base area as Comilla.

I took a jeep and went to introduce myself at the nearest Field Ambulance at Allagappa. There most of the talk was shop and local gossip – bubonic plague had been diagnosed at Chaung-U, a village not far away; a Gurkha soldier had just been admitted with indigestion which his MO thought might be due to his having eaten a rat. I found the MO who had been with the anti-tank regiment before me; he was now MO of the 1st Devons. We talked of trivial things; I did not ask about the work.

Back at the Regiment I sensed that the arrival of a new MO was not looked on as a good omen. The men's work was over for the day and, seeing a motor-bike, I asked if someone would teach me to ride it. They all would. No problem until I wanted to stop; no one had told me how. After several circuits through bushes and cactus one of the laughing men ran alongside and told me what to do. It took our minds off the days ahead.

I had at my disposal eight stretcher-bearers under Bombardier Lang. They were mostly Devon men, slow, solid, friendly, capable. As well as being expected to carry the wounded and apply dressings and splints they looked after the general arrangement of my Aid Posts and took care of the medical stores. Drugs, dressings, surgical instruments, splints – everything needed for the first crude treatment of the seriously wounded – were in one large box that could be carried on a mule or in the back of a truck. In another box was the usual supply of medicines for the day-to-day treatment of minor ailments, and in a third were 'Medical Comforts', the best known of which were a few bottles of spirits.

My bedding was unrolled for me that first night in a shallow pit, and I found my personal belongings – mug, knife, fork and spoon, tin hat and a steel ammunition box in which I had a few books and papers – arranged nearby within reach. Alone, I had time to think about the immediate future and before it was dark I wrote a couple of short letters. One was to my mother; I tried to put in it the love I felt for her, without giving her any reason to worry more than usual about me. The other was to a friend of both of us, and to him I quoted Milton's Samson – 'Happen what may, of me expect to hear, etc', saying that I wished I felt like Samson. No lights or noise were allowed so near the river and soon all was dark and silent. I felt at home and among friends. I lay awake a good deal hearing from time to time the crackle of small arms fire, sometimes far, sometimes nearer, and wondering if it meant anything for me. I reflected that whatever lay ahead I probably had only myself to blame for being where I was.

Gracey's plan for 20th Indian Division was that one of its three brigades should cross the Irrawaddy near Myinmu and gain a footing opposite. A second brigade was to do the same a few miles downstream. These two brigades would make a firm bridgehead which would entice the Japanese to attack in strength.

The Division's third brigade, hitherto in reserve, would then also cross into the bridgehead and break out to the east to lead a 50-mile drive by the whole division to Kyaukse.

Kyaukse, 25 miles south of Mandalay, was on a main road and railway and its capture would add to the dislocation of Japanese communications in Central Burma which Slim meant to bring about by taking Meiktila. These plans, like Slim's larger plan to take

Rangoon before the rains, were of course unknown to those like me who lived from day to day and moved under orders.

On the morning of the second day before the crossing I was at Regimental Headquarters when Jumbo, who was now Acting CO, came to me with my orders. I was to go with Major Haden's battery of three-inch mortars that would be firing at targets on the bridgehead from Satpangon, a village on our side of the river three or four miles from Allagappa. There were a few houses at Satpangon and some pagodas damaged by shellfire; the river bank there was in general high and steep but close to the village a rough track led to the water's edge and Satpangon had been chosen as the embarkation point for the first troops to cross. Weapon pits for our mortars had already been dug near the pagodas; the position was screened by a few trees from the river and from the far bank, but it was likely to be shelled when the enemy pinpointed it. Jumbo had a knack of making you feel that your job mattered and that he cared personally about your fate. He said he wanted me to be with the battery that was going to fire from the village from which the crossing was going to be made;

"It'll make a hell of a difference to have you there. I hate doing it straight away like this, Doc, when you've only just come, but it'll mean a hell of a lot to those blokes." He added thoughtfully, "You'll be shelled to buggery."

I warmed to old Jumbo and would have jumped to do anything he asked. I collected what kit I thought I should need and went to introduce myself to the Battery Commander. Bill Haden was a schoolmaster by profession, gentlemanly and reserved, much liked and respected and known to the men as Major 'Aden.

We moved off before dusk and parked our trucks for the night on open, uneven ground a mile and a half from the river bank. Some gunners put barbed wire round the camp; the need for secrecy made us speak in low voices. After dark a supply party started for Satpangon; some had mortars on their backs and pulled behind them a handcart full of mortar bombs. They shuffled off in the direction of a lane sunk between high banks. It was a relief when someone handed me a mug of tea. A dog howled in the

Pagoda
Satpangon.
Near Myinmu.
7eb 1945

village, then all was quiet again. The minutes passed with great slowness. I leant against a jeep and stared at the stars, Orion in a clear sky, but my mind was up the lane. Half an hour passed. There was no reason for anxiety except that all was so new to me. Five minutes later there was a dull explosion.

"That's near where they are." I asked what it was. "A grenade." A whispered argument followed. "Was it one of ours or one of theirs?" Had they run into Japs or into one of our own patrols? We waited, all on edge. Another half hour passed, the silence broken only by whispered conjectures. Then a scared-looking officer appeared and gave us news: a grenade had been thrown from the bank at the side of the lane and had just missed the handcart of mortar bombs. Five men were injured and when they limped back I had them helped into the back of a covered truck. We let down the canvas flap so that no light showed when I examined them with a torch. Three, including the Battery Sergeant Major, were bad enough for me to want to get them to the Main Dressing Station at Allagappa. If I had had more experience I should have told the Battery Commander that I could look after them where they were till daylight and they would do very well, but I told him that they ought to be at the MDS and he at once drove them to Allagappa in his jeep. The night was dark and it was quite possible that he might run into Japs: we knew that there was at least one party of them prowling about on our side of the river.

Two hours later he was back, having had no trouble, but we heard next morning that during the night eight Indian soldiers had been ambushed on that same bit of road. I slept under a tree near one of the trucks, pistol by my side, and the rest of the night passed quietly.

In the morning, hidden by long reed-like elephant grass, we moved up on foot to join the rest of the Battery at Satpangon. The heat was trying and I had a feeling that we were moving inevitably towards the edge of events that one part of me dreaded. The first troops were to cross the Irrawaddy as soon as it was dark. An irritating jig which I could not stop kept running in my head: "You've had it. You've had it, you silly old bugger, you've had it!" There was no comfort for me in reminding myself that I had got into this job by my own meddling.

I found a pagoda with room enough inside for me to use it as my

Regimental Aid Post. There were several pagodas like it; they stood on square plinths and were 20 or 30 feet high, white, round, tapering – in their way, I supposed, beautiful. Some had been damaged by shells or bombs, and bits of plaster, rubble and gilded ornaments lay about on the ground. A few steps led up to each pagoda and low white-washed walls, now partly destroyed, surrounded them. Inside, on a sort of altar, was a Buddha about twice man-size, flanked by two smaller plaster figures kneeling with hands raised palm to palm in adoration. There was room enough inside for four of us, and while my three stretcher-bearers, Lofty Freeman, Dolbear and Payne, were setting out the medical gear I went out to look about me and to let everyone know where I could be found when needed.

All about us men were making final adjustments to the placing of their mortars. The range to targets across the river might be two to three miles and they were going to use some new long-range mortar bombs for the first time. The bank beyond the screen of trees fell abruptly 30 feet to the water's edge; the stream ran smoothly at two to three knots; on the far side, nearly a mile away, I could see a shelving beach. Beyond it the land was low-lying and covered with straw-coloured elephant grass. Here and there dark green patches marked clumps of trees – villages. All was unbelievably quiet, peaceful. From the pagodas a track led down to the water and I found it difficult to believe that three weeks earlier, almost to the day, twenty-four cornered Japs, weighed down by full equipment, had committed suicide here by marching straight into the river. The hot afternoon passed slowly. All I could do was sit about, read a bit, write a note now and then and talk and listen. Sitting on some rubble under the placid eye of a Buddha on a plinth in the open I heard how cider was made on Devon farms. "Thar i'nt any drugged ztuff, 'tis the real thing, Zurr." By then we were so hot and tired that there was no tension in the air.

"'Ere's Major 'Aden, Zurr." The Battery Commander was going round his men. Dark haired, of medium height, rather stocky, a calm, solid sort of man, he was absolutely imperturbable. A scholar and a bit reserved, I wanted to know him better. He sat down by me and began to fill his pipe – Wills Cut Golden Bar I thought, I must see if he has any to spare; other men's tobacco always smelt better than my own tasted. He wore no shirt and I noticed a big scar where his left kidney would be; it must have been an ugly wound – shell splinters, I later discovered, at Bishenpur, in the previous year's battle for Imphal.

"You know, Doc," he turned towards me, "they're a good lot of chaps but . . . well, sometimes in a hot spot you can give them an order: it's urgent – you know what I mean – and what happens? It has to sink in; he has to think about it, then he says, 'Ar, I zee what you mean, Zurr. Ar, Ah'll do that.'" The Major, detached in a way as I was, a spectator of himself and of all that went on around him, was all the time measuring the honest efforts of the citizen soldiers doing their best in a world strange to them. He was measuring their efforts against the professionalism of the regular soldiers with whom we lived and fought – Gurkhas, Indians and what remained of regular troops in the British battalions. "These chaps of mine, doc," he went on, "insist on doing what they've been taught is 'a prarper jarb', and a 'prarper jarb' is oiling and polishing their beloved guns, not messing about with 'ranging' and 'bearings' and all that nonsense."

When he left to go on with his round, I thought about my own small section. I had already found that quickness was not their strong point, though they were quick enough when it came to wondering whether someone was being funny at their expense. They reminded me of the advice never to be funny until you had first made friends, and "never, ever, to be funny with the Regimental Sergeant Major". I was beginning to get to know and like them; they were anxious about their mates with the anti-tank guns who would be going over the river with the infantry and would be close to the enemy when fighting began. "It's deadly," they said when something was bad. When it was past endurance – the ultimate horror was – "deadly". It might rarely be "fucking deadly", but not when they were in earnest; then it was just deadly.

Mugs of sweet milky tea came up, gloriously hot tea that made the sweat run off us in streams a few minutes after drinking it. There was everywhere a sort of false calm. One of the gunners lying on the ground in front of me, his mug of tea between his hands, suddenly looked up and said, "We'm right 'appy yurr, Zurr". Later came a shout of "Karner's up" – 'Karner', the British soldier's mangled version of the Urdu for food. A gunner brought me a plate of stew and some biscuits; we shared the night's issue of rum and at nightfall took our places in the pagoda, stretchers propped in a corner. There had been fighting here in the past month and as darkness fell I began to notice the sweetish smell that rises at night from the bodies of the dead.

When it was dark men of the Border Regiment filed silently down to the water's edge and began to cross; they were followed after midnight by a battalion of the Frontier Force Rifles, and the battle of the Myinmu bridgehead began.

I did not try to keep a day-to-day account of what happened during the next few days; they passed, a mixture of fear, work and long waits. I was sometimes on one side of the river and sometimes on the other. I jotted down notes from time to time on odd scraps of paper. I wanted to remember everything. The waiting in the pagoda at Satpangon seemed interminable; it was hot even in the shade inside, but infinitely worse in the glare outside. In the pagoda I sat looking at Buddha, clasping a half-empty tin of bully beef and a packet of biscuits; one of his plaster acolytes wore Payne's bush hat tilted at a rakish angle. Around us on the floor were half-empty mugs of tea, crawling with flies. My Red Cross haversack ready for going out to the wounded stood beside Buddha on the 'altar'; Sten guns belonging to Dolbear, Payne and Lofty Freeman were propped against the pagoda walls. The stretcher-bearers I had met at Regimental HQ belonged to other batteries and were on the bridgehead with gun crews. As we listened to the battle developing we wondered what was happening to them. Now and then, to make conversation, I would say, "Well, Lofty, tell us how you enlisted," and if anyone came into the pagoda we would push over a packet of biscuits and say, "Sit down – cut yourself a piece of cake". Our mortars were firing day and night as called for, and so was Corps artillery from farther back. We were shelled a little in the mornings and evenings and I got to know the sounds of the Jap guns and the low rhythmic whirring of shells coming our way. From over the water came the noise of small arms, of different kinds of machine gun. The men identified them for me: "That's an LMG, Sir" (Light Machine Gun). "There's one of our Brens. Listen." "Medium Machine Gun now, Sir," and so on. Bangs of all kinds came from different directions as attacks and counter-attacks were mounted, grew in intensity and died away.

There were large numbers of Japs in the villages and long grass on the other side of the river; I watched what was called 'softening up'. Squadrons of Liberators flew over and plastered the ground with bombs. Hurribombers followed and did an air-strike on a tiny village without a name just across the river from me. I wondered how anyone with imagination could possibly take it – or, for that matter, give it. It was horrible to watch at close quarters. Sometimes I felt hollow inside and I could feel my heart thump; my mouth was dry and above all there was the fear of showing any sign of fear. To have work was a relief, because, when idle and waiting, we had time to brood. We felt resentment at blunders which killed or wounded our own men, and resentment against those high up who had no bond of sympathy and understanding with us but sent us to places and expected much of us. I was grateful for the loving kindness of Jumbo and the soothing outward tranquillity of 'the Major'. I hoped desperately that the MO too was displaying a soothing outward tranquillity.

Watching my companions as I sat outside the pagoda in the cool of the morning or went round the men as they worked on their mortars I noticed how, during the quiet after a few shells had dropped, one of the Troop commanders, a lieutenant, talked far too much and his men doubled the quiet obscenities that were part of their daily speech. So they made the formless terror we all knew seem less important than the defined immediate discomfort or nuisance.

One morning when I was cleaning my teeth I looked up at aeroplanes overhead and was startled to see red discs on their wings: they were Jap fighter-bombers – Oscars. Surprised, we all scrambled into slit-trenches. They dropped a few bombs and used their machine guns but did not do much harm.

After dark on the second night I stood by the track that led to the river and watched a battalion of Gurkhas going down to the boats. They were an impressive very solemn little crowd with white tapes sewn on their behinds so that they would not shoot each other by mistake in the dark. Instead of the usual cheery smile there was on each face a look of grim purpose.

The nights were the worst times, the times of most tension. We four in the pagoda kept watch in turn for intruders; when it was my turn I dozed off and woke at intervals with a guilty start. The slightest noise made us wonder. What was that? Who was it? To pass the time the men told in low voices tales about waiting in ambush at night in the Kabaw Valley.

"We used to call it Death Valley. There were no birds there. We'd sit waiting in the dark for them to come down the track and one of those damn great leaves – you know, Sir, off the teaks – would drop and you'd jump out of your skin. Then you'd settle down again and listen once more to the drip, drip off the branches."

Now and then beleaguered troops being attacked in villages on the bridgehead called for defensive fire and the whole battery would blast off with stunning noise a salvo to destroy Japs forming up to attack. Behind us the Corps artillery thundered and flashed in the dark night. By day, to while away the heat of the afternoon, I listened to a Troop Commander describing the individual Jap as a fanatical and desperate fighter who would keep going until his ammunition or his body gave out. He told me about the mortars and said that, when firing at ranges up to 2,500 yards, they were accurate enough, without dropping bombs on our infantry, to destroy Japs forming up outside a village that we occupied. Later I was to recall and doubt his assurance.

When I went over the river to visit gun crews in the villages I crossed on rafts powered by outboard motors. The rafts were made of beams and planks laid across iron pontoons which the Japs had used as assault boats. The first time I crossed I shared one of the pontoon rafts with several soldiers and two mules. As soon as we left the shore the mules gave trouble and a British soldier and

I climbed off the planks into the end of the pontoon to get as far away from them as possible. One mule glared round showing the whites of its eyes and unsteadily backed a hind leg down into the pontoon a few feet from us; we each put a leg over the side, ready to slip into the water. It was the kind of thing that took away any romantic feeling I might have had about rafting across one of the great rivers of the world. The crossing took twenty minutes. On the far side I found what was sometimes called 'a bit of a huddle', the beach busy with the landing of men, guns, mules and supplies.

Only in one place was there the outward appearance of calm, a small oasis of quiet where an MO from the Field Ambulance had set up an Advanced Dressing Station. It was in the shelter of the bank where the level of the land dropped a few feet to the shore. A tarpaulin had been rigged to give shade and several soldiers lay quietly on stretchers waiting their turn to go back over the river. The MO was bent over a man half stripped to show a shoulder torn by a shell. The images of that day stayed for ever with me – the stuff of a doctor's nightmare: a beach where a canvas stretcher was the operating table, the grey clammy skin of the shocked man, a race for life between blood plasma pouring in and the bright blood pumping out, an artery somewhere deep inside. I did what I could to help and went on to look for my gunners.

The bridgehead was in a gentle bend of the Irrawaddy where the river which had run west from Mandalay for 40 miles turned south-west towards Myingyan. The ground was flat and sandy, and covered with elephant grass. It was seamed with sand-filled *chaungs* or water-courses, at that season dry. In the bend of the main river were several small villages, not one of them more than 300 yards from end to end: Yekadipa near where I landed, Lingadipa half a mile downstream, and Kanlan, Gaungbo, Talingon and Sinbyugon all slightly inland but none more than five miles from the river. To gain and hold the bridgehead, the Division had to capture these villages and then hold them against counter-attack, and each village in turn became the scene of a minor battle or series of battles. Names like Sindat (Elephant camp) and Talingon (Threshing-floor) which might in happier times have conjured up images of tranquil village life came to have dreadful overtones and lingered as names of bitter memory in the minds even of men who were hardened to war. There were fires everywhere and a column of smoke meant the site of what had been a village. In hamlets that lately had been leisured and smiling, as I had seen Sadaung, I picked my way between slit trenches, bunkers, wire and all the litter of battle. Trees were broken and houses destroyed and charred, and in the air lingered the stale wet reek of smouldering fires; it mingled with the stench of the dead.

In the confusion of noise and movement and rumour I was often surprised by islands of stillness where, in low voices over mugs of tea, a gunner and I would talk of his home, his family. There I could write, or read, or dream, and share with another as much of myself as I chose. These unreal calms were due not so much to pauses in the fighting as to the movement of action, now here, now there, so that a man might find himself suddenly remote from it and willing to withdraw for the moment into a remembered or imagined other life. Some incidents, either because they were macabre or painfully close to us, were special, like watching a section with flame-throwers burn Japs out of long grass or out of bunkers; others were absurd, like listening to the wireless news. The BBC were always good for a sour laugh when you were yourself at the place described. On 18 February we heard on the wireless that there was "a new beachhead west of Myinmu". "The first crossing," said the voice, "was made by three swimmers; rafts powered by outboards followed, planes roaring low overhead to drown the noise of motors." The only swimmers of whom we knew were some whose raft overturned on a sandbank, and we were sure that we had heard no "planes roaring low overhead".

Some of the fiercest fighting on the bridgehead centred round the two villages Kanlan-Ywathit and Talingon, which were occupied by the Frontier Force Rifles and Gurkhas respectively. Anti-tank guns with these battalions formed part of the perimeter defence of each village and there some of our gunners became casualties when the Japs attacked in force on successive nights. Two gunners were killed defending their 6-pounder when their position was overrun at Kanlan-Ywathit; the gun was recaptured in the morning when, out of 179 Jap bodies counted on the perimeter, it was found that thirty were in the area immediately in front of the gun. On the next night four more gunners were killed and four wounded at Talingon with the 4th/10th Gurkhas. Their gun also was overrun in the night, but the sergeant in charge was able to remove the breech-block, making the gun unusable by the enemy. That gun too was recaptured in the morning and put into action, although the Japs had fixed a mine to it and stuffed the barrel with grenades. The fighting round these villages was very fierce and close-to: take, re-take and take again, and at Talingon alone when at last the village was cleared on 26 February the Gurkha battalion which had held it counted over 500 enemy bodies. I did not hear anyone during those days using the word prisoner; it was not a word in anyone's mind. No one expected if overrun to be taken prisoner and no one expected any Jap to let himself be taken alive.

A week after the first crossings the battle had moved out of range of our mortars at Satpangon and I moved to the bridgehead for good. The Mad Mullah was now back with the Regiment and he set up what he called Tac HQ – Tactical Headquarters – half a mile south of the river near a small village which on our map had no name; it was about half way between Yekadipa and Alethaung. The CO, Adjutant, RSM and a few signallers and drivers would be at Tac HQ and I decided to stay there too as it was a convenient centre. We were a dozen in all and lived in slit trenches. The ground was flat and the soil dry and sandy. We had a bit of barbed wire round the camp. At night I felt naked on this bare open patch of ground; except for the wire we had no defence. At dusk and before dawn we stood to, armed, tin hat on, alert for a surprise attack. Every evening, waiting for the first shot of a 'jitter party' to ring out, I watched Venus in the sky over the barbed wire and wondered if anything dreadful would happen before the planet was out of sight. For some reason I found nights at the unnamed village tense, each of the first three worse than the one that went before. Yet nothing happened. I thought 'jitter' a very expressive word; a 'jitter party' was a small patrol sent out by Japs to harass with random shots, grenades and sometimes shouts. They made the inexperienced tense and worried; sometimes positions were given away by returning the random shots. When all was quiet I listened for sounds outside the wire. Was someone there? Half a dozen? Fifty perhaps? No one at all? One night as we waited and listened a lonely voice out of the dark cried, "Help! Help!" He was a lost swimmer from 2nd British Division which was crossing the

Irrawaddy higher up near Mandalay. Someone fetched him in. He had been seven hours in the water.

I shared a trench with the CO at Tac HQ. There was more space in it than in a slit-trench and when we came down after stand to on the first night Steve, the adjutant, joined us. He produced a bottle of gin and I had chocolate from home to share out. After the CO had taken some tobacco off me to fill his pipe we started to talk. The trench was five feet deep and big enough for three or four to sit together; during the time I shared it with the Mad Mullah I got to know this strange man a bit and up to a point to like him. "I have always," he started off, "got what I wanted, Doc. Made a point of it, you know." He was one of the two children of a widow and was, I suspected, rather spoilt, for the other child was a girl. He was tallish and very slight and had "always been a good athlete – boxer, polo-player, pig-sticker," though to me he did not look it at all. He had a lean hungry face, light brown downy hair and light blue rather prominent eyes. He was brisk and testy in manner, conceited, dogmatic and condescending. His brain was lively enough but he seemed to have no idea of what his officers and men were thinking and feeling. I was surprised when he told me that he had "more experience of handling men than anyone else in the world," for he harassed and interfered with those under him, until they were wildly exasperated.He didn't bother me much for he confined his advice to me on medical matters to saying, "Must see they get vitamins, Doc. Get them to dig up peanuts. Plenty of them in the ground. Get them to dig up peanuts."

For two more weeks the battles for the small villages continued. The CO in his jeep visited in turn the villages where there were anti-tank guns manned by his men. I had no jeep of my own so I went with him; he sat in front with the driver and I sat behind with his bodyguard, Busty Peacock, a large amiable man with a Sten gun. I had by now exchanged my revolver for a rifle, with which I was more at home. By day there were many quiet spells and I saw more of Bill Haden. His battery was near Yekadipa and I found him there sitting on the edge of a slit trench, unruffled as usual, measuring every enigmatic word he uttered, and systematically reading through his India paper airmail edition of *The Times* which was delivered with his letters.

"Look at these chaps, Doc." He gave a slightly incredulous

laugh. "Absolutely ordinary blokes, citizen soldiers, and yet they treat in a totally matter-of-fact way days and nights of killing and being killed." I enjoyed the relaxation of his company and we did a lot of talking, but I discovered very little about him then, except that he too had been at Oxford, at Wadham. How far away now all that was! I began to jot down absurd and banal comparisons on little bits of paper – Oxford and Yekadipa, the Cherwell and the Irrawaddy, leisured speculation and crude slaughter. My real life had contrasts enough without such imaginings, one minute admiring the kingfishers and terns sweeping and hovering over the river, the next doing what I could for a wounded man; one day stealing to the river with some gunners and a few grenades to catch fish for our dinner, and the next at Talingon viewing the heaps of blackened half-digested Japanese corpses. On 27 February the 1st Battalion of the Devons relieved the Gurkhas at Talingon and brought bulldozers to dispose of the bodies and clean up the place. I watched the Gurkhas march from the stinking filthy village where night after night for a week they had repelled the fiercest attacks; they might have been coming off some ceremonial parade, they looked so spick and span, their uniform cared for and their weapons clean.

East of our camp near Yekadipa was a village called Sindat. When the Border Regiment took it they were supported by a troop of anti-tank guns and I went with them to a point where, from the shade of a thorn bush, I could see what was going on. I could see a dark-robed figure in the open, sometimes crouching, sometimes moving on; it was a Roman Catholic padre, a man always to the front, respected by all, and now during the attack giving comfort to the dying.

When I could I sought the shade of trees, but except in villages there were few trees on the bridgehead. February was the middle of Burma's dry season between the cool months and the hot season, and although I was too cold to sleep at night after 5 am even with a pullover and blanket, by noon the temperature was already creeping up towards the 100 degree mark. But the climate was not uncomfortable: the air was dry and, in spite of the heat, I found that I had plenty of energy to dig a slit trench. To be near the river was a delight – sweaty and dusty, we would strip off our clothes and swim, and when we had done that and thrown in some grenades we would go in again to collect the floating catch. At night, back in the trench at Tac HQ, as we listened to battles round this or that village I heard more about the CO's early life. He told me how as a subaltern in India he ran a pig-sticking club; he said that it was a point of honour with pig-sticking clubs to chase any animal they flushed: one club was disgraced because the members refrained (very sensibly, I thought) from chasing a tiger they put up. I had to admit that dull and conventional as many of the British I had met in India had seemed to me, there was a fine tradition of courage and personal honour.

The Mad Mullah could be friendly when he wanted to, as when one night he said to me, "Doc, you old cockyolly bird, I think you're rather enjoying yourself here, aren't you?" He was right, of course, for I wrote home at the time, "I can't say much about my job except that there have been moments more satisfying than I could have ever imagined." Although there was boredom at times (no one in the Army escaped that) the job opened my eyes to what the men put up with and said very little about, something I could not have understood without sharing their life. There were plenty of minor ailments to treat but my usefulness was more in being present than in anything I did; it was in being with the men, advising occasionally about little things and being available in case of serious injury. The life of movement suited me, and the life in the open. I learnt about people and about myself; it was amazing how many friendships sprang up under those conditions and did so quickly; a man very soon got to know on whom he could and could not rely. I found that physical fear was not so formidable to me as fear of censure, fear of admitting that I wasn't as good as I wanted to be. I could remember being more frightened of making speeches than of anything on the bridgehead.

On 1 March our rear echelon crossed the river and the whole of Regimental Headquarters assembled and got dug in near the village of Bethaung close to the river, a little to the east of where I first landed. Early in the day I had been looking down at one of our lads after a medium machine gun killed him. Moments earlier he had been a young man I knew, full of go. I hated the black holes with ragged edges, the torn skin grey like putty. I hated death by machine gun. In the afternoon I borrowed the Padre's jeep and took Bombardier Lang with me to Kanlan and Yezin with medical stores: that morning there had been a scrap there. On the way I heard that Colonel Whitehead, CO of one of the Gurkha battalions, had been killed by a stray shell and I had a vivid picture of watching him earlier as he calmly directed affairs from a low ridge near the beach, but any ridge was conspicuous in that flat land.

On 2 March we were shelled at RHQ during the night and the CO was more than usually fussy in the morning. The Regiment took his ways very hard. The presence of this unpopular and eccentric meddler seemed to me to irritate nearly everyone. I got on well enough with him because his meddling in my affairs was trifling and well-meaning, and consisted only of telling me to encourage everyone to eat corn on the cob, young beans and peanuts, of which there were plenty in the ground. At RHQ my men dug and roofed a small bunker that would do for a four-bedded ward – that is, it would take four stretchers; it only ever had one patient in it, the CO. When we had finished the bunker we took the rest of the morning off to go swimming and fishing. Two handsome kinds of black tern could always be seen flying backwards and forwards over the water at that place. One was small and graceful, and had a black belly. Drawn up on shore were a number of country boats beautifully built of teak. Near them a bull terrier called 'Gunner' belonging to one of the Battery Captains was busy making advances to a lovely golden setter called Sue. She, all silk and grace, belonged to the Adjutant, Steve, who was very fussy about her and always insisted that she wore specially constructed baffling drawers when she might be on heat. As I lay idly on the sand I could hear the swish of the terns' wings, and the low voices of the men 'effing' and 'blinding' without emphasis. It was one of those intervals of quiet in our lives.

Next day the CO came to me in the evening for a pill. He had stomach ache. He called me again at 2300 and I thought he might perhaps have appendicitis. At 0330 he called me once more so I moved him to my roofed-over sandy dugout to look at him with a torch. He was a bit worse and as by now he had taken more pills I got a jeep and took him over the river to the Field Ambulance. Two Gurkhas came with us as escort and we reached Allagappa at 0600. John Bruce, Consulting Surgeon XIVth Army, happened to be there and took out the appendix at 0800, after breakfast. All was set out in the big tents of the Field Ambulance as in any operating theatre in a civilian hospital, and the atmosphere was much the same. Only the patient was tense. Bruce did his best to make him relax by relating an old chestnut about lying back and enjoying rape. The joke got him nowhere with the Mad Mullah who gave him a suspicious look. As the anaesthetic began to work, I watched, fascinated, a last admonitory gesture of the Mullah's right arm and hand, forefinger characteristically outstretched and pointing as even there he laid down the law.

I crossed back over the river during the morning and found that Jumbo had assumed command. I felt that already perhaps I had done a good day's work. In the afternoon I went on to Yezin, taking the Padre with me. We had mortars at Yezin, and fighting was still going on in places along the south-east limit of the bridgehead, roughly from Sinbyugon to Mayogon. I meant to stay the night and before dark we did some digging to deepen a bunker for our own protection. The Regiment also had mortars and guns at Mayogon and Kanlan, and next morning, 5 March, I visited them too before returning to Bethaung.

When I got back to Regimental Headquarters at 1530 I noticed a big man with red tabs on him talking to Jumbo. It was my ADMS who had come to say that I was to leave the gunners right away and go to Sinbyugon as MO to the Devons. According to the ADMS they had had a bad time in the last few days with shelling and mortar fire and their MO had been posted elsewhere. "I want the best chap for them I can lay hands on," he said, "a tough MO who will stand no nonsense." His words pleased me and made me uneasy at the same time, like when Jumbo said it would mean a lot to the men and we'd be shelled to buggery. They were good at handling people, those two. I hurriedly packed my belongings, borrowed a jeep with a driver to bring it back, and by 1700 was at Sinbyugon.

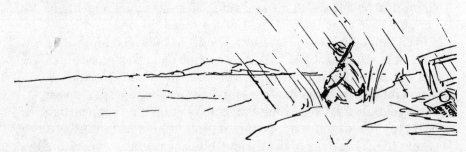

Chapter 10

The Devons (1)

"YOU'D BETTER GET over there right away" had made me wonder what I should find; Sinbyugon was very like other villages I had seen, a few smoking bamboo houses, a clump of trees, some trenches and a lot of wire. I said, "I'm the new MO," and I was shown into a large dugout which was covered with a tarpaulin so that lights would not show. Colonel Jones was a tall, thin man with a stoop; he wore steel-rimmed spectacles and looked ill and harassed. He might, I thought, be an obstinate man. He was standing with his company commanders and others, going over the orders for an attack at dawn on a village to the east of us. They were grouped round a table on which a map was spread, looking at it by the light of a hurricane lamp; outside in the open it was already beginning to grow dark.

I missed the friendly welcome I remembered having had from the gunners. These men were busy and worried. The battalion had been under fire off and on for the last seven days: it was not to be expected that, in the few hours between recovery from making one attack and getting ready to launch the next, they would have time for a stranger, a new MO, but I thought all the same that I had landed amongst a queer lot. I had already been told that I was to take the place of an MO who, after a night of shelling during which there had been casualties in his Aid Post, had said that he could not go on. Morale in the battalion was supposed not to be good and the sick rate was high. I had been told that I was not only to look after the wounded but to cut down the numbers sent back each day because of complaints that were due mainly to fear and strain.

The village we were to take in the morning was Nyaunglebin; we were then to move on to Paunggadaw, three miles to the south-east, and take that as well. I needed to know about the plans so that I could make my arrangements to receive casualties, and I asked a few questions. I had to decide where to put the Regimental Aid Post and make sure that others knew where it would be. After hearing the plans for taking Nyaunglebin and Paunggadaw I chose a suitable place and told the CO. He did not disagree. Did he care, I wondered. He left it to me, without comment and I went off to look for the MO's staff. They must have been wondering if I was going to show up at all.

The next day's attack was to be the start of the break-out from the bridgehead, the beginning of the advance which was to take three weeks and bring the Division to the outskirts of Kyaukse, forty miles on.

The Devons had been stationed in India for fifteen years and some of the men had been out east a long time. The battalion had been in Burma and Manipur since the beginning of 1943, first in the Kabaw Valley and later in the jungle-covered hills between Palel and Tamu. It was one of the battalions which fought on the Shenam Pass and 'Nippon Hill'. Afterwards it had helped to clear the jungles round Ukhrul and in the autumn of 1944 had been withdrawn for a rest. At the end of 1944 it had returned to Burma with 80 Brigade when 20th Indian Division began to move south to Monywa and into the country between the Chindwin and the Irrawaddy.

New men had come to take the place of those lost by illness and enemy action; the CO of the days on the Tamu Road had gone, as had many others, including the MO. Many officers, NCOs and men remained, veterans of the previous year's battles, men who remembered the weariness and the sickness and the ferocity of hand-to-hand fighting; but there were also many new to war, men for whom a few recent patrols and a skirmish or two had been their only preparation for the battles of the bridgehead and for the encounters with Japanese who were on the defensive and well dug in.

After the meeting under the tarpaulin I went to make myself known to the MI Room staff, as they were called. There were more of them on the establishment than I had had with the gunners. Sergeant May was senior, then two corporals and nineteen others, most of whom I attached as stretcher-bearers to individual companies as there was need, holding back one or two at the RAP to help me and Sergeant May. I also had a batman who acted as one of the RAP or MI Room staff, and I had four jeep ambulances with drivers. Two of these belonged to the battalion and two were lent by the American Field Service. One of the AFS men was Dinwiddie Smith from New Jersey whom I already knew; he was a small boat sailor who did something on Wall Street. The other was The Reverend Custer Watson, a very young man whose heart was in the right place but who later provoked me to say, "For Christ's sake, man, put that Bible away and bandage his wounds; he won't need the Bible if you stop the bleeding." Danny James of the AFS had been so exasperated by him that he complained, "Can't he wipe that silly grin off his face and call me a bleedin' son of a bitch or sump'n just once? It'd ease the tension."

Each jeep ambulance was fitted with a steel frame to carry two stretchers, one above the other, and there was room also for someone to sit behind the driver. I always tried to keep two jeep ambulances at the RAP so that I could send the most urgent cases quickly to the rear.

An important member of my section was the battalion water corporal, a stout-hearted laughing man called Stoffles, who wore a peacock feather in his bush hat and was in charge of the water-cart. He was responsible to me for seeing that the battalion was supplied with water which, whether he got it from the village well or from a convenient stream, was properly disinfected with chlorine, using the Horrocks Box, which I now met in use for the first time. I had not seen one since I left Crookham.

Sergeant May was my right-hand man. He was short, wiry and

thin. He wore steel-rimmed glasses and had a peaky face. He was a Londoner and in politics an outspoken Communist. He was an intelligent, bitter man of 27 with no illusions and no toleration of the weak-kneed or neurotic. I thought this rather a defect but it was very useful to me in sorting out the genuinely ill from the faint-hearted and from those likeable old soldiers who were not quite malingerers, but liked to see just how far they could go with their new MO. Sergeant May knew every man in the battalion. We got to like each other and I greatly respected him. He knew his job and the other men respected him too. That first night all I could do was to explain to him what we should be doing next day.

Before first light there was a bit of a scare: a patrol reported Japanese tanks in Nyaunglebin village. This was a false alarm; they were tanks which had been destroyed by Hurribombers a few days earlier. They were derelict and Nyaunglebin was clear. We moved off at 0600 and later I and my section – ambulances, equipment and a few men – had a long wait in the open while the leading company cleared Paunggadaw two miles farther on. I found some shade at the side of a small bush by a tuft of elephant grass. The day was very hot and I felt sick. To pass the time I started to read a pocket *Hamlet*. A letter from home fell from between the pages and I re-read that instead – it was easier than *Hamlet*. Shells began to fall on the track behind us and later, when we had moved to Paunggadaw, on the village. It surprised me how many could fall without anyone being hurt.

The country before us to the south and east was gently undulating and did not rise anywhere more than 600 feet above river level. The earth was hard and in places there was rock near the surface. Except for low scrub, thorn, cactus, sisal and in places what might have been the remains of a crop of cotton, the land was bare, like desert. Sandy paths led from village to village and the ground was criss-crossed with small water-courses or *chaungs* which in February were dry. The *chaung* at Gyo, which we did not reach for several days, was as dry as the rest but much wider – about a quarter of a mile across and deep in sand. Farther on, as we drew near Kyaukse, the country became flatter and had more appearance of cultivation; there were irrigation canals and one or two metalled roads.

In the first two days we crossed a range of low rocky hills; they were brownish yellow in colour, dry and stony. The highest point was a triangulation mark, 486 ft, which acquired a momentary importance in our lives because it had to be taken, although there was no one actually there to take it from. Patrols and stray villagers from time to time reported large numbers of Japanese in front of us, and we called down on them concentrations of artillery and mortar fire. An air-strike by Hurribombers was asked for on the first day and May drew my attention to the dozens of vultures which afterwards circled overhead. "Fresh meat tonight," he said drily; he believed that the vultures knew from experience what an air-strike meant for them.

During those days I lived alone with my own group, the MI Room staff. We slept and ate together, and were our own companions and intimates. Each night the adjutant gave us an area to ourselves and there we dug slit trenches as a precaution against night attack. As a rule one trench was for two men and I usually shared a trench with my batman. I kept my bedding and such odds and ends of kit as First Aid haversack, rifle, tin hat, washing and shaving gear and eating utensils above ground at the side of the trench. If there was a convenient tree we hung the *chagals* or canvas water-bottles from it to cool the water; if there was no tree we hung them on the front of a jeep. I normally slept rolled in a blanket at the side of the trench and we did without mosquito nets because they got in the way if one had to jump into the trench. Some belongings which I did not want to lose, like books and a chess set that often entertained us (I had bought it for five rupees in Calcutta), I kept in an ammunition box that was stored in my jeep. The area given us when the battalion stopped for the night was usually near Battalion HQ: at the end of the day I could be found there by anyone who wished to report sick. Apart from battle casualties, with which I dealt as they happened, there were always a few men with fever, diarrhoea, sore feet and vague complaints which might or might not be serious. These last, and the overall picture of how many were going sick for trivial reasons, needed my constant and careful attention. The only officers of whom I saw much at that time were the CO and the adjutant, Captain Holwill. He was a young, dark, sturdy fellow of about my size, with a small black moustache. He was usually quiet of speech and I thought him a good bloke;

he knew his job and always did what he promised.

On the night of 7 March we met as usual at Battalion HQ for the evening Order Group and heard the latest Sitrep – information about Japanese in villages around us. Next day the battalion was to take the village of Kanma, four miles farther east, with the help of tanks which were expected from a place called Magyi, a village to the north of us. The day started with an air-strike and more vultures; then there was a long wait for the tanks to appear. We marched over a rocky, stony ridge through thorn-scrub and cactus until we were about a mile short of Kanma. Here a message came back to say that Kanma was more strongly defended than expected. I set up my RAP and we started digging in case we should be surprised and shelled. Digging in the heat of the afternoon was a desperate business; in the stony ground it was difficult to get down more than a few inches and we worried all night about not having proper cover from shells and mortar bombs. Corporal Stoffles, wearing his Gurkha hat with the gay peacock feather, appeared with the water-cart at tea time and was very welcome. We poured the water into galvanized iron *pakhals* that fitted in a jeep or on the back of a mule. A *pakhal* held about five gallons and was convenient for filling the water-bottles and mugs of the thirsty men. The days in early March were beginning to be hot and on one of them I made a note, "85 degrees in shade at noon". We started giving out salt tablets as a routine for the men to put in their water-bottles; the more impetuous swallowed them two at a time and were promptly sick.

In the end it was a battalion of Gurkhas that took Kanma and we did not enter the village until first light the next day, 9 March. We then had to wait while companies cleared villages on each side of our track onwards to Gyo. During the wait a Jap prisoner was brought in, the first any of us had seen; he was not wounded but he looked very thin and pale; his hands were tied behind his back and a BOR with a fixed bayonet walked just behind him. Not long afterwards a Burman from the village climbed a toddy palm to change the gourds in which they collect sap; the juice seeps from cuts made in the stalks of the fronds at the top of the tree. It was a curious statement of everyday village life going on in spite of us. When at last we moved on I came across a badly wounded Jap in the open; he had a compound fracture of the thigh. We put him on a stretcher and carried it back past some of our men. They were waiting to go forward and we ran the gauntlet of an unending refrain which infuriated me: "Bring the bugger here, Sir. We know what to do with him." The Jap was so very ill that I was provoked to tell them to "fucking well shut up and you're damned lucky not to be on stretchers yourselves", and a lot more for which afterwards I was sorry. My reaction was reflex, mechanical, the doctor looking after his patient, whoever he might be. Several times afterwards I heard joking threats to prisoners not very seriously injured. I took no notice except to see that treatment was not skimped. Before I left the Devons wounded Japs were being brought in on stretchers and given cups of tea because they were now the underdogs.

Later in the day I took two jeeps to pick up some casualties in open country to the south of the track to Gyo, and in a dip of the ground came across a Japanese 105 mm gun in a sunken lane. I stopped the jeep and went on foot with one of my stretcher-bearers to have a close look; we had an absurd temptation to hook it to the back of the jeep and tow it into camp. "Look, even the Doc's section's brought in a Jap gun!" Then the stretcher-bearer muttered that it might be booby-trapped and I realized that we were behaving like children; our job was to pick up wounded men half a mile away. I sent someone back to report our find and the rest of us went on. We stopped that night about a mile short of Gyo and dug our slit trenches in very hard ground.

The Devons took Gyo on 10 March. Two companies moved off at 0400 and crossed the wide chaung to the west of the village to make flanking attacks, but were held up at first light by machine-gun fire. At 0845 a third company with tanks attacked the village directly and by 0915 HQ Company had advanced to the west bank of the chaung. By noon Gyo was clear of Japs. We crossed the chaung near one of our tanks which had been hit and was still burning and entered the village along a sandy lane that was about six feet below the general level of the surrounding land; I set up the RAP there to take in casualties from the battle that was going on beyond Gyo. As my jeeps came over a low rise near the burning tank a 105 mm shell landed behind them. More shells followed and soon they were landing about one every fifteen seconds all over the place. The area about the village and up the lane was stiff with trucks and men. Where the lane was deepest I made some fellows move their jeeps to make room for mine so that the RAP could be in the most sheltered place. While I was doing this one shell landed in the sand, smack next to my own jeep, destroying my pack and its contents, which happened that day to include the precious chess set. Strangely, no one was hurt and the jeeps were not put out of action, though two of them afterwards looked like pepperpots. We parked them up against a sandy bank where they were pretty safe.

The RAP staff had all been too near the last shell to be happy, so I dosed them with small amounts of brandy and then did the same for some members of HQ staff who looked as if they needed the treatment. Patients do not care to be attended by doctors who smell of drink, but apart from that and the fact that it would not have looked well for me to be seen tippling, curiosity about myself at such a time forced on me a self-denying ordinance where drink was concerned. Several more shells came over but nothing else at the RAP was damaged. It was the first time I had been shelled in the open and it was most unpleasant. Soon we began to deal with casualties from the battle half a mile ahead of us. I was at Gyo until the evening, by which time we had packed all the wounded off to the rear. We made a brew of tea and then followed the main body to a village called Ywatha about three miles farther on.

I arrived there in a jeep driven by Dinwiddie Smith of the AFS; we came over a low rise and saw on our right, on slightly raised ground, some of our men in slit trenches; others lay in firing positions on an open slope before them. To our left were clumps of trees and a row of palms. Machine guns and rifles were firing. On hearing that one of our men had been hit by a sniper I stopped the jeep. I could see the man on the open ground before us and I heard a shout, "They've got him". I took the words to mean that someone had got the sniper. I was in that sort of careless exhilarated state that sometimes came over me after a day when I was keyed up, and without thinking I said to Din, "Right. We'll pick him up." Din drove on without hesitation and with help from two men who appeared from nowhere we carried the casualty up a slope. We put down the stretcher behind a low bank while the men kept on firing at the trees with Brens. When I examined the 'casualty' I found that he had not a scratch on him; when someone had fired from the trees he had been so surprised that he had simply dropped on the ground, paralysed with fright. He was quite incoherent and instead of giving him a piece of my mind as I felt inclined I gave him a big dose of morphia to keep him quiet; next day he was perfectly all right.

Before digging in that night we counted thirty-four Japanese dead. We were on a low hill a little short of Natthadaw, surrounded as usual by a perimeter of wire, slit trenches, and men on guard with Brens firing on fixed lines along the edge of the perimeter. At dusk we stood to in the usual way and ranged our mortars about the perimeter in case of attack in the dark. Small bush fires were started by the mortar bombs and lit up the drifting white smoke and the silhouettes of toddy palms against the night sky. As soon as it was dark our area was mortared and shelled for a short time by the enemy, but except for one burst of Bren-gun fire the night was otherwise quiet. Patrols went out in the small hours and on returning before dawn reported many Japs at Gwekon and Tanaungain and in the country between. About midnight, soon after the burst from the Bren gun, I was roused to attend to one of the men. We had a general rule that no one ever went outside the perimeter in the dark, except for patrols whose times of going out and coming in were known to the sentries. This man, wanting to relieve himself, had carelessly wandered out into a Bren-gun's fixed line of fire. He was badly cut about and was lucky to be alive. I patched him up and sent him back to the Field Ambulance in the morning.

A young and agreeable man, Captain Spread, joined the battalion at Ywatha and took Holwill's place as adjutant. It was 11 March; the Frontier Force Regiment passed through our area and for the next week took the lead in the advance. They ran into Japanese opposition half a mile farther on. We at Ywatha were subjected to sniping and several men in the camp perimeter were wounded; after first aid treatment they were sent back as soon as the track was reported clear. The battalion was then ordered to put a road-block at Gyo, now behind us, and the company that went back to do this reported a concentration of 300 Japanese north of Taungledaw, a village three miles south-west of us.

In that sort of war there was no such thing as a stable front, as it was understood in static warfare. We were advancing from west to east, moving so many miles each day and taking village after village but leaving on either side of us villages which might sometimes be occupied by Japanese. Each night we leaguered in a village or camped in the open, and were ready to be attacked from any direction. The track behind us was often shelled or attacked by Japanese. We sent patrols to villages on either side of the road, and often found they had to be cleared of the enemy, sometimes for a second or third time. There was no question of drawing a line from north to south and saying that we were on the west of it and the Japs on the east. It was more as if one were to draw a line from west to east and say that at the west end of it we were in the majority, though there might be a few scattered Japs, whereas at the other end there were more Japs.

For the infantryman not in battle one day is very much like another. His march starts early in the cool before sunrise; he swings along at the side of the dry dusty track; on his head is a bush hat, over his shoulder his tin hat and a rifle or Sten gun, and on his back a cluster of odds and ends, usually including a 'brew can', a blackened old tin with a wire handle. In front of him, through dust clouds raised by passing jeeps or guns, he sees a shambling figure which is a replica of himself. At the side of the track are dust-covered trees, dry sandy ditches and the litter of a retreating army. Scattered about the rocks and fields are the stiff corpses of men and animals, swollen and discoloured. His sweaty tramp is relieved by ten-minute halts, sallies of grim wit and, very occasionally, pleasing encounters with villagers. At last, usually before noon, he reached a clump of palms or a village, throws off his pack and sets about brewing up. Someone shouts, "Chae's up!" and he pours hot, sweet, milky tea into his dried-up gullet, sore and stiff with dust and heat. Out come picks and shovels and the digging of trenches and fox-holes begins.

What he thinks of is always home – green, cool, full of love, womankind, food and beer – his idealized England. And yet, though most seem to have those dreams, they speak cynically about politics and are too disillusioned to think that their dreams will really come true. The dreams represent what they would like, not what they expect.

My routine varied from day to day: a daily sick parade of some kind, a bit of administration and the treatment and evacuation of casualties when we were in action. My kit was the clothes I stood up in, some odds and ends like compass, maps, a few books, shaving kit, rifle, tin hat and water-bottle, plate, mug, spoon, blanket and ground sheet, and so-called jungle boots, rather like basket-ball boots. During the day I became greedy for shade, whether a tree or a bit of canvas, and spent my nights sleeping under the stars, close to a slit trench or bunker. It was a kind of life I found supremely satisfying. I was learning about myself and the job. I found that in tight places I could think fairly calmly and that others would do as I told them. I hated telling men to go where it would frighten me to go, but they had their job and I had mine; often I evaded the problem by going with them. I found that I could work all day in the hot sun and do my share of the digging for a couple of hours in the evening. I slept well when I could sleep at all. I was learning also what the ADMS had meant when he talked to me about the job. I felt that to do it well would need a better man than I. Dealing with battle casualties was only a small part of the work. The part I liked least was a kind of sorting – into those that I thought could stand a bit more and those that could not. Lord Moran wrote in a book about a very different war that "the wounds we dress are as nothing" compared with the hurts of the mind.

But there were compensations too. One evening after a day of fighting which had still not died down a soldier came to me for some small attention. He was not a strong man – he was in a way one of my problem children – often coming with vague and trifling complaints which made me suspect he was trying to work his ticket. That night he was a very different man. He was happy, eager, and a bit talkative. His eyes were bright; he was like someone who has found a treasure. He had found that he was worth something. He had, so he told me, himself killed three Japs: "One over there, Sir, one there and one there. What happened was . . ." and so on. The Japs may have been half-starved but the point was that the fight had exalted him. He seemed innocent. A week later he was himself again but I never forgot that glory of his that recalled Julian Grenfell's poem,

> And when the burning moment breaks,
>   And all things else are out of mind,

And only joy of battle takes
Him by the throat, and makes him blind.

As an RMO I was lucky enough in those days to have work that
had meaning; the life was exciting and my companions good. Until
we can look back we rarely know enough to say, "This, now, is
fulfilment"; but I think I must have been very happy then in a grim
fashion. I realized afterwards that my attention was often directed
more to those not wounded than to the wounded. The wounded
were leaving the scene and for them I could do no more. My
services to them had been important for the sake of those who were
still in the fight, and it was to those in the fight that my attention
must be directed.

On 14 March we were at Chaunggwa in company with a battery
of guns when thirty BOR reinforcements joined the battalion. In
the small hours of the next morning one of our patrols starting out
in the dark was shot up by one of our own sentries: one BOR was
killed and two wounded. It was the kind of misadventure, due to
failure to pass on information, that had a very bad effect on morale.
We passed Dwehla next day and reached Ngazu where there was
a bridge over the Panlaung River. The bridge had been damaged
and needed repair before the tanks could cross. The Frontier
Force were dug in on the far side of the bridge, and next day were
expected to go on to capture a road junction at Nyaungwe, three
miles farther. There the Devons were to take over from the FFR
and to advance to Kyaukse, another four miles.

My RAP at Ngazu was by a small pagoda. When I arrived two
wounded Burmese were brought to me on stretchers, a man and a
young girl, both with broken limbs; they were victims of the
shelling. The camp perimeter was not many yards away and drawn
up near me was a troop of tanks. Their heavy machine guns
pointed over the wire and along the road, a deadly threat to anyone
approaching from the east. I had been warned that fighting patrols
had gone out to villages north of the road and would be returning
before dawn but the tanks did not seem to know; the fog of war
was not confined to great battles and offensives – it crept with its
doubts and uncertainties into the littlest skirmish.

On 17 March we reached the road junction at Nyaungwe and
moved into the Frontier Force Regiment's positions. From

Natthadaw we had come 25 or 30 miles. Next day patrols were to clear the road north and others were to occupy the village of Ngedo which was wrongly supposed to be empty; without tanks in support an attack was not pressed.

We were at Nyaungwe for five nights and on the first day we made contact with 32 Brigade which was to the north of us. I had a chance to chat with the MO of the Northamptonshire Regiment. He was a small, phlegmatic, determined individual who told me how he dealt with men who complained about their feet. "I sit down by the roadside, take off my boots and socks and say to each one, 'If your feet are worse than mine I'll do something about it, but if not, you can get on with your job.'"

Colonel Jones and the adjutant visited 80 Brigade HQ at Dwehla and came back with a new 2 i/c, a tall, capable-looking man, Major Freeman Mitford; they brought orders for our next moves. The first village on the Kyaukse road, Puttaing, was partly occupied by the enemy, and there were Japs dug in by the road itself and in the villages on either side: Pahtodaing, Zegon and Thinbok. On the 20th an attack was mounted against Puttaing after an artillery bombardment, but the attack was called off in the absence of tanks and in the face of medium and light machine-gun fire. That night the enemy fired thirty rounds of 75 mm shell into the area of battalion HQ.

I had a sizeable RAP at Nyaungwe. We roofed it with baulks of timber covered with a good deal of earth so that casualties had protection from the nightly shelling. We were jittered throughout the night of the 20th and another thirty rounds of 75 mm shell fell inside our perimeter. The 21st was a bad day. Large numbers of men were reporting sick all day and cholera was suspected in the area; as well as dealing with men going sick I paid a quick visit by jeep to the ADS near Brigade at Dwehla to get cholera vaccine with which, during the day, I injected all those in the battalion whose cholera immunization was due. The numbers reporting sick continued high all evening and at seven that night one of the men shot himself in the hand. I had seen too many self-inflicted wounds, usually in the foot. What could you do about them? I dressed them; they might have been accidents. But rifles and revolvers do not go off by themselves (unlike Sten guns, perhaps) and the position of the wounds in the hand or foot and the man's attitude to it, a mixture of fright and satisfaction, made me suspicious. I wrote them down as accidents, not as self-inflicted wounds, and I took care not to publicize them. The man's companions always knew what had happened. They knew the man concerned and were slightly contemptuous but not censorious. I never noticed that a self-inflicted wound had a bad effect on others; they were only sorry that a man had been brought to do this to himself. My attitude was that the sooner these men were out of the battalion the better.

One of the draft that joined at Chaunggwa was a youngster who had not long come from Somerset. He was by me one night at evening stand-to and talked to me about his home. His way of speaking reminded me of the Devon men in the Anti-tank Regiment:

"Where'm you to, Zurr?" (Where do you come from?)

"'Pick 'ee oop', E zed to Oi." After a while I suggested that he might like to have a talk with the Padre about his problems and heard him mutter to himself, after a little thought, "Ee, Oi caan't stoomach'ee."

Neither could I, as a matter of fact; he struck me as wet and pi, as the saying was. I was not feeling very good myself that night. I had no thermometer because the breast pocket of my tunic was so hot in the middle of the day that the mercury repeatedly burst the glass. After breaking several thermometers I gave up carrying one and I now got Sergeant May to take my temperature – 101 degrees. My left hand was swollen because of a septic sore and I was bothered by the diarrhoea and nausea from which we all suffered in small doses from time to time. These ailments were no more than those for which I treated others all day.

At midnight the jittering began. There were brief attacks on our perimeter, shouting, the use of dischargers which lobbed grenades into the battalion area, and a good deal of fire from an 81 mm mortar. In the morning we found that the Japs had left nine dead bodies and one wounded man on our wire. I was up intermittently all through the night as casualties were brought in. Just before midnight thirty more rounds of 75 mm shell were fired into the battalion area but injured no one. Our casualties seemed to be mainly from grenades and rifle fire, and sometimes from our own mortar shells falling short.

Lieutenant Watts, a very good officer who had been a long time with the battalion, was brought to me that night. The front part of his head had been blown away by a mortar bomb and he was in a bad way. I had him put into the bunker and after dressing his wound I sat by him for a while listening to his breathing. In two hours he died. I felt the more bitter from believing that it was one of our own mortars that had killed him. At dawn the sporadic attacks and the sniping were still going on. Behind us the road to Dwehla was being shelled and was too dangerous from sniper fire for me to send casualties back.

Chapter 11

The Devons (2); Kyaukse

FROM OUR POSITION astride the road junction by the canal at
Nyaungwe I could see Kyaukse four miles away. The town was at
most about two miles long from north to south and a mile wide
from east to west, but it was bigger than any town we had yet seen
in Burma. Kyaukse was important because it was on the road and
rail route between Mandalay and Meiktila; it was a main Japanese
supply depot and a link with their armies in the south; the Japs
meant to hold it as long as they could.

As I looked from Nyaungwe the country before me was
absolutely flat to beyond Kyaukse where a hill dotted with white
pagodas rose abruptly to over 800 feet, the near end of a rocky spur
of a range of hills visible in the distance. I could see very little of
Kyaukse itself for it was screened by trees. On the plain before it
were a surprising number of small villages marked by clumps of
trees in which the white tops of pagodas showed. The road to
Kyaukse ran in an almost straight line and was lightly metalled:
the surface would bear motor traffic and even tanks. The hard
surface was not much wider than the width of one of our big trucks
and on each side were the dusty earth tracks used by bullock carts;

136

the paddy fields, at that season firm and hard, were at a slightly lower level.

As I looked along the road the Tamok canal was on my right or south side, and for a mile ran parallel with and not far from the road; then, at Zayat, among trees and a few pagodas, the canal turned north, passed under the road (Zayat bridge) and made a loop to the north that took it half a mile from the road before it turned south, crossed once more under the road (the 'second' bridge) and continued south to Myaung U. After that the canal ran south-east to Letpanbin, a village on the outskirts of Kyaukse.

The canal was very like an English canal – the sort of thing you might find in Shropshire – but shallower because it was intended for irrigation, not navigation. The road bridges across it were simple arches, generally made of brick, and because the canal was below road level they were not hump-backed. The distance from Nyaungwe to Zayat was a mile and from Zayat to the second bridge, another mile, the general direction of the road being a little south of east. From the second bridge south along the canal to Myaung U was rather less than a mile, and from Myaung U eastward, again along the canal, to Letpanbin was also a little less than a mile.

When the CO and adjutant came back from the 80 Brigade conference at Dwehla on 21 March we met for a final Order Group. The CO explained that tomorrow the battalion would take Zayat and go on to capture the second bridge. After taking the bridge we would dig in on the east side of the canal. There would be air support and support from tanks and artillery.

It was a bad night, with shelling and repeated attacks on our perimeter, and in the morning I wrote in a notebook:

"March 22nd, 0830. All hell began ahead – planes, tanks, artillery. Dealt with a number of wounded, and realized that as the road behind was being shelled and was also subject to small arms fire from both sides, I could not at once send casualties back to the ADS at Dwehla. About noon I took a trip forward to see what was going on."

At 0830 D Company had attacked, with a troop of tanks in support, and soon afterwards had taken Zayat bridge. The Japs had blown the bridge and Bailey bridging was sent for so that the tanks could cross the canal. The morning's action brought fire from Thinbok village and at 1030 A Company attacked with tanks and cleared two villages, Thinbok and Zegon. Meanwhile the enemy began to shell the area of Zayat bridge.

At 1330 C Company moved forward through Zayat and went on to take the second bridge; by 1430 they had taken it and orders came for the battalion to consolidate at the second bridge on the east side of the canal.

At 1500 I collected my section and moved up; we passed through Zayat and went across the open stretch to the second bridge. Above the general noise of battle we could hear the loud crack of bullets as they passed, and Sergeant May's jeep was hit, but without serious damage. When I crossed the second bridge I found that to the left of the road on the far side of the canal there was a dyke a few feet high that ran parallel to the canal. The dyke was several yards from the canal bank and I chose a hollow in between as the place for my RAP for the next bit of action as the battalion closed in on Kyaukse. We began digging.

The battalion was now concentrating near the bridge and the enemy fired six rounds of HE into the area. When I looked back along the road I saw a jeep get a direct hit and go up in flames. I jumped into my jeep and, thoroughly frightened, started out for the scene; halfway there someone stopped me and said that miraculously no one had been hurt. I was thankful and at the same time for some reason felt slightly deflated, perhaps after having screwed myself up. I returned to the RAP where Sergeant May already had everything organized. Seven Japanese bodies and various bits of equipment were lying about the area and soon we were dealing with our wounded, dosing them with drugs, attending to their injuries and seeing them comfortably on stretchers until it was safe for a jeep ambulance to take them back to Dwehla. In the meantime some Japanese opened up with a battalion gun from a position north of us, among the trees by the canal.

Half an hour after I returned to the RAP two anti-tank Quads towing guns and carrying ammunition received direct hits near the place where the jeep had been hit half an hour earlier, just south of the road and halfway between Zayat and the second bridge. An agitated Troop Commander stood before me. He wore a green slouch hat, his open-necked green battledress blouse was untidy and his trousers above brown leather boots hardly came down to

138

his ankles. He had popping eyes and a sort of wispy moustache. He looked a mess, distraught, clutching his empty tobacco pipe. His Quads, the means of using his guns, were being destroyed and the two guns lay useless in the paddy. His Troop was finished. "Ten wounded men," he said, "and four dead. Can't you *do* something?"

I took two jeep-ambulances to 200 yards short of the burning Quads and went on foot to see if there was anything I could do. On the road were two Lee tanks, their guns banging off at intervals with a deafening noise. They were shooting at something in the woods north of us, perhaps the battalion gun. Standing by one of them I looked up and spoke to the Tank Commander; he was in his turret and said that he had been searching with glasses and could see nothing moving by the Quads, no wounded; by now the Quads were a blazing mass, the ammunition they carried banging away all over the place. The Troop Commander came up to me and asked me to go on with him to the Quads and call on my jeeps. I refused either to accompany him or to send my men. Words which I have now forgotten but which greatly angered me passed between us and he walked off to the blazing trucks alone. A jeep with two anti-tank gunners came up to me and I recognized Dolbear from Bill Haden's battery; he had been one of my stretcher-bearers at Satpangon, and I told him to take his jeep, at a safe distance from the exploding ammunition, to make sure that there was no one lying out wounded in the paddy field beyond the trucks. Later I found that in the first Quad that was hit three gunners sitting on the bench behind the driver had been killed outright by one armour-piercing shell – solid shot. No one else had been seriously hurt.

I walked back to my own jeeps and we returned to the RAP. Shells were falling near the second bridge and I was in time to deal with four casualties as they were carried in. One was a Company Commander, Major Douglass; he had been very badly injured and lost the greater part of one hip. He was not properly conscious as he was carried off the road into the RAP and I saw that he could not last long. We dressed the wounds as best we could and a Corporal called Sargent and another jeep-ambulance driver were able later to get the wounded back through Zayat to the ADS without incident.

That night I talked about Douglass to Captain Holroyd who was now in charge of the Company. Douglass was a man I had much admired and had thought one of the best of the Devons' remaining officers. Holroyd, a steady sort of man, told me how Douglass had shouted, "Stretcher-bearers! in that awful way they do after a shell has dropped".

One of the other companies was short of stretcher-bearers and after we had eaten in the evening I told three of my men to report to that company. They were good men, but they had had a heavy day and before they would go I had to speak to them more sharply than was usual for me. Their names were Young, Herford and Scully.

During the early part of the night Sergeant May and I shared a hole we had dug in the west side of the low dyke that ran parallel to the canal. We crouched side by side, pressing back at intervals into the earth burrow for shelter, and he told me about his London background. After a while he dug his paybook out of his breast pocket and took out a folded letter to show me. It was from his mother: "Dear Stan, can you send me a snap of you outside your bungalow?" We were able to laugh and then get some sleep. At two in the morning the enemy began a series of attacks on our perimeter, keeping up a steady bombardment of the battalion area with grenades from discharger cups. They kept it up until after five in the morning when they made their last attack and withdrew, leaving one body on our wire and a trail of blood going to a nearby village. During the night defensive fire from our own mortars had killed one of our men and wounded several more. Seven men were carried into the RAP; one died there three hours later and the others I recorded as "fair to middling", but one of these died later at the Field Ambulance.

Patrol reported that during the night Japs had come back to occupy four bunkers on the south side of the road between us and Zayat and had also come back to re-occupy the copse north of the Tamok canal and not far from us; it was there that they had the nasty little piece of artillery known as a battalion gun which was much hated. In the morning I had for a time to keep all the wounded at the RAP because the road was no longer safe for ambulances; however, I was able to send them off at about one in the afternoon.

At 1430 a 75 mm gun began to shell the battalion very accurately. A few minutes earlier there had been a shout of "Karner's up!" from the cookhouse. One of my stretcher-bearers had picked up his mess tin and was about to step on the road when he heard the sound of the first approaching shell. I heard him mutter, "O fuck the karner," as he dived into the nearest slit trench.

Spread, the adjutant, and his batman were both hit about 20 yards away on the Kyaukse side of the bridge, where they had begun to dig a slit trench at the side of the road. Jock Heaney, one of the best of my stretcher-bearers, ran forward with me to see if we could do anything for them. The batman had multiple injuries of which the most in need of attention was an artery in his upper arm that was spouting blood. It was easy to stop that and Jock Heaney, with another stretcher-bearer who had now emerged from the RAP, carried the batman back while I went to look at Spread, crouched on his side, poor little devil, in the hole he had only just begun to dig. Fortunately, though he was not yet dead, he was unconscious. He was gasping for breath at long intervals in a way which made me think of a sobbing child. As I tried to assess the extent of his injuries – he had taken the full force of the explosion – I heard more shells coming and without knowing what I was doing found myself face down in a puddle of water at the side of the road, so quick were my reflexes by now. Then Jock Heaney was back with a stretcher and between us we carried Spread to the RAP.

Jock Heaney was a specially good bloke who, like Sergeant May, was one of my chief helpers in the RAP. He was a medium-sized, black-haired Glaswegian, aged 27, a widower with a little girl. He was a Roman Catholic, quick-witted and slightly slow of speech. He had lived a lot in England and spoke more like a country Scot than a Glaswegian. He was well built, handy with a spade and friendly. He had only recently volunteered as a stretcher-bearer. Before that he was a fighting soldier. He came back one day from fetching in a casualty with the American, Din Smith; Jock was scornful of the men whose company it was: "They wouldn't budge from their holes," he said, "not even to fetch in one of their own."

At five in the afternoon I was brought a message to say that three of my stretcher-bearers who were with one of the other companies had been killed by a shell that morning: Young, Herford and

Scully. I went to investigate and to check the names: it was true and those were they. They were killed outright. A direct hit, I was told, probably a 25-pounder. The stretcher-bearers, whether at HQ or out with the companies, knew each other and were a close, friendly group. Young, Herford and Scully usually went about together and they had two particular friends at the RAP, Macey and Stevens. The two were so broken by the news that I knew that for a while I could make no use of them. "Why can't they stop?" cried Stevens, "God! Why can't they stop?" I hardly knew the three dead men but coming on top of the events of the last few days their deaths shook me too. Stoffles, the usually cheerful water corporal with the peacock feather in his hat, sat on the ground with his head in his hands, saying, "I can't stop thinking about them". I kept thinking of Spread as I had found him, crouched where he had been digging, his breath coming in little gasps that sounded like sobs. None of us wanted food that night. They were days after which we needed comforting, but all my mind would do was to go over events and wonder if I had shirked anything.

The third night at the second bridge I noted as a quiet night, but Japs were prowling round the perimeter. There was small-arms fire on and off all night and before dawn a wounded Jap was found abandoned by his companions – an unusual event. He was taken prisoner.

Patrols that had been out during the night reported Japs at the two villages Myaung U and Magyidan, on each side of the canal, less than a mile south of us; at midday a patrol on the east bank of the canal reported both villages clear and the battalion was ordered to move at once into the Myaung U – Magyidan area. I packed up the RAP at the second bridge and began to move my section down the west bank of the canal to set up an RAP at Myaung U. I had just been told, "No medical arrangements called for – the area is now unoccupied" when there were urgent shouts from the direction of Myaung U for "Ambulances – Stretcher-bearers!" As usual, I thought.

Japanese with medium and light machine guns were still stubbornly occupying bunkers in the east part of Magyidan and as I moved down I began to meet casualties. On the canal bank short of Myaung U was a jeep-ambulance on which lay our new Second in Command who had joined the battle a few days earlier. Major

Mitford had a bullet through his neck and when I looked I found that the stretcher-bearer who had picked him up and put him on the ambulance had done as good a first aid job for him as anyone could. He was lucky and later made a good recovery. I set up the RAP near a pagoda on the canal bank at Myaung U as more casualties came in, and here news came that I had lost one more stretcher-bearer.

Lewis, a young man whose home at Dolgellau in North Wales was not far from my own, had gone into the open near Magyidan to bring in a casualty. He knelt to put a field dressing on the wound, and then lifted the man on his back. When he stood to start the carry he was himself shot and killed. The wounded man rolled to the ground and lay for some time in a hollow before crawling to safety. It was only a few days since Lewis and I had sat for half an hour together, talking in Welsh about scenes familiar and dear to us both.

Digging that evening beside the canal, we found that we could not dig deep because canal water began to seep into the bottom of the trench. I moved the RAP in among a small cluster of pagodas enclosed by a low white wall. A drink ration was issued; mine was a quart bottle of warm American beer. There were tamarind trees by the canal at Myaung U and when the evening breeze stirred the leaves it stirred also the tiny temple bells; they gave out a sweet tinkling as they must have done for hundreds of years.

The day that followed began with heavy shelling of the second bridge where we had been for the last three days and nights. The Frontier Force had moved in there and I heard that one shell fell exactly in the middle of where the RAP had been. Perhaps it had not been a good idea to have put it so near an obvious target like a bridge.

At Myaung U we were shelled in the afternoon and evening by 75mm and 150 mm guns with surprisingly little effect, but our forward platoons suffered greatly from small arms and machine-gun fire. They were now up against the last line of the Japanese defences of Kyaukse. The enemy was well dug in before the villages of Mezebin and Letpanbin. I was able to treat and send back by ambulance a number of seriously wounded men, but was much more worried by the very large number that came back to the RAP suffering from nothing more than nerves: most of these, after I had listened to them and sometimes given a placebo, I sent back to their duty. Among them was one of my stretcher-bearers who had been carried back sobbing and had had to be soothed and returned to the company from which he had come. Another stretcher-bearer had run away during the night and could not be found. Among the wounded was an Indian soldier who had had a bullet through his head from side to side and, contrary to the popular belief that a bullet through the head is fatal, was surprisingly full of life.

The demoralization of the many unwounded who went sick was a bad sign, but not all the unwounded who came my way were demoralized. I wrote of one man, "The wretched Shippey came in tonight seeing his mate's face everywhere." Shippey's mate had been shot but Shippey carried him from where he had been shot until he found he was carrying a dead body. I sat with Shippey for a time and later, when he had settled down, he fumbled in his pockets and produced a pair of Japanese forceps he had picked up, saying, "I knew I had something I had to give the Doc." Someone else brought me a beautiful, small, compact case of Japanese surgical instruments which he had picked up at a position his company had overrun. Other trophies from positions that were overrun were art nouveau – contemporary drawings in black and white of 'comfort girls', anatomical details imaginatively picked out in scarlet. These specimens were only on show to us and were not given away by their owners.

Plans were laid to make a final attack on the Japanese positions on 27 March, which was to be supported both by air and by tanks. At mid-morning there was heavy bombing of the Japanese positions but without success: the supporting tanks got bogged down in a marsh; one of the attacking companies was pinned down by machine-gun fire and by late afternoon it was clear that no progress would be made without heavy casualties; 80 Brigade HQ called off the attack. Next day there was more heavy bombing of the Japanese positions by the RAF: Thunderbolts bombed and strafed them in the early afternoon and Hurribombers repeated the onslaught later; the Japanese were still there in the evening after an artillery concentration had been brought down and the Devons made no headway.

An exception to the low spirits of the men was to be found in an

144

old regular Warrant Officer, Sergeant-Major Streak who after a few drinks exposed himself recklessly to enemy fire in a brave attempt to take a position on the canal bank half a mile east of Mezebin village. There may have been many individuals like him but the battalion was now in no condition to do more than send out offensive patrols. The Japs still clung to their positions on the outskirts of Kyaukse. We were visited by the CO and IO of the Northamptonshire Regiment and there was some talk of that battalion relieving the Devons. In the event the Japanese made the decision for us on the day that our relief was being discussed.

The 9th/12th Frontier Force Regiment had bypassed Kyaukse on the north and taken the 800 ft high hill immediately over-looking the town. Japanese resistance ended and an evening patrol reported Letpanbin clear; at dawn next morning Mezebin too was clear. The enemy had melted away into the hills to the east of Kyaukse and except for abandoned stores there was nothing in the town.

When I woke before dawn on 30 March I was lying on my blanket on the brick floor at the side of a pagoda. I felt unac-countably low, sensing that a special time was at an end. It was odd how flat one felt after the action – half longing to be back in its unpleasantness and excitement. Din had pleased me one night when, frustrated, I had said that I sometimes wished I were a combatant officer, and he said, "Gee, you'd do that all right."

I remembered lying there the night before, happy after the day's work, stretching tired limbs and dreamily aware of the small pagoda in the corner of the low-walled enclosure. The moon rose and flooded it with light. I could hear the low voices of the signallers at their sets, and the familiar jargon. "Star, is that Star? Crete line here. O.K. Sir, you're through to Star."

The fleeting time of stand-to in the morning was beautiful; the sky was dove grey, the moon not set, and the great tamarind tree by the canal, its leaves turning colour, stirred in the wind like English trees in autumn. I was happier then. The cool fresh breeze that swayed the palms and made the temple bells tinkle blew away my spasm of morning gloom. I wished that in sketches I could do justice to the beauty of the countryside, centred round clumps of trees and largely depending on artificial irrigation. My surround-ings at Myaung U were lovely, a little village with a cool artificial

145

waterway running through it, shady trees, grass almost like English grass, and palms, a well, a grove of banana plants and the pagodas by which I lived. It was Good Friday. I walked into Letpanbin and the Northants marched into Kyaukse.

I went to Evening Service on Easter Sunday; I did not quite know why. About one eighth of the battalion was there, sitting in a half circle around a clearing, a grove of palms on one side, the canal on the other. It was a hot sweaty evening and the sentiments expressed by the Padre and by the Rev Custer Watson bored and embarrassed me – the acceptance of a benevolent deity. I wished at times that I too could accept such an absurdity and I was surprised at how many British soldiers, unreligious in their lives and in their thoughts of every day, were superstitious and credulous when it came to religion. Custer read, or quoted, "Yea, though I walk through the Valley of the Shadow of Death" with a distressing American accent and with painful attention to emotion. Only the final blessing carried conviction, whoever it might be addressed to; "Be with us all, and with those whom we love."

The next few days were better for the battalion. The men were having some rest and I had a chance to inoculate most of them against typhoid, tetanus and cholera, an outbreak of which was confirmed by the doctors at the Field Ambulance at Dwehla.

We turned the pagoda forecourt into an MI room. Sergeant May and two helpers set up a trestle table and stationed me there with a fully loaded 10 ccs syringe of vaccines; the men were paraded by companies and filed past. Each man's paybook was inspected before he reached me to make sure that he was due for injection and another of my orderlies made a note of the fact after the injection was given. Someone kept me supplied with fully loaded syringes and I put a dose into each man's arm as he passed. The men were in a good mood, beginning to relax from the pressure and strain of the last weeks and as the companies filed by with their left arms bare, sleeves rolled up, I realized that they were quietly singing. The tune seemed familiar, *Pistol Packing Momma*, and gradually I made out the words, "Lay that needle down, Doc, lay that needle down."

Chapter 12

The Race for Rangoon

AT THE BEGINNING of April the Devons moved to Pyiban, a mile south of Kyaukse. The battalion, with other British infantry, was to be withdrawn to India and I expected to be posted to some other unit in the Division.

When not in action my men made a habit of sleeping on spare stretchers which they found easier than the hard ground. On our first morning at Pyiban one of them complained that something under his stretcher was moving and making a rustling noise. A small crowd gathered to watch while two men suddenly turned the stretcher over and exposed a large snake. It was brown, thick-bodied, and 8–10 feet long – a rat snake, not poisonous. But the BOR, like the Indian soldier, looked on every snake as bad and this one was quickly despatched with a blow from a heavy stick.

All of us in our different ways had been for weeks and months on 'The Road to Mandalay' even if it was not Kipling's 'road'. I had not thought it possible that Mandalay would be disappointing and would leave me bored, but, except for the thrill of expectation as we drove past hundreds of pagodas, the town was dull and in ruins. I would have exchanged it any day for an untouched Burmese village. Much of the Fort and the central part of the town was destroyed, so we drove on to look at Mandalay Hill, the great rock which stands on the north side of the town. It was 700–800 feet high, covered with shrines and bearing the scars of battle. The climb to the top, up hundreds of steps, was hot and tedious.

From Pyiban I paid visits to the nearest Field Ambulance and on one of these visits I took the CO with me. He had been ill for some time and I had at last persuaded him to be properly examined and treated. I suspected that he had amoebic dysentery and at the Field Ambulance they decided that he should be sent back to India without delay.

About the end of the first week in April there was a change in the weather pattern and on 12 April I was driven south through a rainstorm to rejoin my old friends of 111 Anti-tank Regiment. They gave me a lift in convoy to a place six miles south of Meiktila; one of the 20th Division's Field Ambulances was not far away and I went there to ask about my next job. I had no wish, if there was any choice, to return to a medical unit and I asked the ADMS, who was there, if I could not remain as RMO, say in a Gurkha battalion. He said that he would have to use me in a British unit and that it would have to be the Gunners – 114 Regiment, RA. We had become friendly and when we were alone after a convivial evening of poker he went back briefly to business: "Those Devons," he said brusquely, "you stopped the rot." Remembering the last days before Kyaukse, I wondered if he was not overstating the case.

XIVth Army was now moving south along two lines: 4 Corps down what was called the railway corridor east of the Pegu Yomas; 33 Corps, to which 20th Indian Division belonged, down the Irrawaddy Valley to the west of Pegu Yomas in the direction of Magwe and Prome. 20th Division was to intercept Japs retreating east across the Irrawaddy from south-west Burma and the Arakan.

I joined the gunners in time to take part in what Slim called 'The Race for Rangoon'. This stirring phrase did not refer to some neck and neck dash by competing elements of XIVth Army for the honour of being the first to capture Rangoon; it did not even refer to a race

148

between our overland invasion of Burma and a possible seaborne invasion mounted from the Bay of Bengal. It was, more prosaically, a race to seize the deep-water harbour of Rangoon before monsoon cloud and rain made the supply of an army overland and by air impossible.

I caught up with 114 Field Regiment, RA at Natmauk, between Meiktila and Magwe. It was a place where there were large numbers of captives – Japanese prisoners and surrendered Indian National Army (for the most part Indian soldiers captured by the Japs earlier in the war and induced to change sides). They were herded together in a huge compound in huts roofed with bamboo, an enclosure which had served as a hospital. The Japanese were emaciated. They lay on the ground shivering with fever and many of them obviously suffered from diarrhoea. They looked at us with empty eyes. Armed Gurkhas stood guard, though this was scarcely necessary because these men could hardly have walked a step.

My new CO was a tall raw-boned man with a bushy black moustache, a strong red nose and a shock of dark hair flecked with grey. He wore his cap tilted well forward over sunglasses and his hair at the back bulged under the rim of his cap and over his collar. He wore the ribbon of the DSO which he had been awarded in Italy. He greeted me with hopeful enthusiasm; "Glad to see you, Doc. Play bridge?" I had to admit that I did not play bridge and his interest waned perceptibly; it always does when you have to confess that you do not play bridge. His name was Mackenzie. I liked him. He was straight, with level eyes. He laughed pleasantly and his conversation was made up largely of 'I mean' and 'What!', words that did not sound at all fatuous on his lips. I imagined him to be a fairly typical good type of regular soldier, fair and sensible. We talked one day about 'non-fraternization' and he said, "It's hopeless with the British soldier if there are children about. I mean, look at 'em, Doc." We were in a village and one of our trucks in convoy was halted on the road, waiting to move as soon as the truck before it moved, and there were children all over it, responding to the driver's advances. In central Burma we had lots of the little beggars about – quiet, smiling and attractive, with brown faces, almond eyes, chubby bodies, jet-black hair.

The gunners struck me as having a professional sort of technical polish of which I had not seen much since my days in hospitals at home, and I quickly became interested in them and their guns, the 25-pounders, one of the most famous guns of the war.

I found that I had taken the place of a Czech psychologist whom everyone treated as having been a bit of a joke, and I thought at first that I should have my hands full. I set the MI room staff to dig slit trenches while I had a long conversation with the bombardier in charge. I liked Bombardier Lawrence and knew we should get on. He was 25 years old, very dark and slight, with a long face and good features; he was intelligent and took a pride in his job. Jimmy Fields, my batman, was a short, sturdy, fair man of about 27; he was a treasure, very good at odd jobs, thoroughly even-tempered, full of fun and backchat, and a good scout. Jimmy had a way with Indian soldiers. He talked vigorously at them in what, as far as he was concerned, was as good as their own language – a string of Urdu words spoken quickly and decisively with much grinning and gesticulation. The words were chosen absolutely at random and made no sense, but the Indian soldiers loved it.

"*Kis Mukkan?*" was a phrase he used as a greeting, without much idea of what the words meant. "*Kis*" meant, near enough, "What?" and "*Mukkan*" "Butter", – "*Kis Mukkan?*" he would say, as you might say, "What cheer?"

The people I most liked and found genuine and interesting in that unit were the other ranks. Whenever I could I ate with them. They were the middle class or lower middle class ordinary folk – commonplace perhaps in their tastes and thoughts, but sincere and often intelligent. There was no pretence about them, and no bad language, a state of affairs attributed to the example of my predecessor but one, a Captain Tannock, who for three years had been MO to the Regiment.

One day I came across Lawrence and Jimmy Fields by the road-side teasing a fine looking Frontier Force Rifleman and a couple of Punjabi Mussulmen. I often felt that the Indian soldier, and not merely the Gurkha, was first-rate. The good battalions of Punjabis, Dogras, Jats and FF Rifles all came into that category. In that terrain and climate those who served with them agreed that they were at least as good as the British soldier. Their own officers of course thought them better than anyone. They had a fatalism and simplicity of needs which helped them to endure continued strain, heat and rough living, and they could carry on unperturbed when the British soldiers I had happened to be with could not.

Life with the Field Gunners was luxurious by comparison with the sort of life I had lived with the infantry and even with the Anti-tank Regiment. For much of the time we were on the move, but we lodged in relative comfort, using houses, tarpaulin shelters and the regimental trucks. My medical gear was kept in the Dodge, in the back of which we put stretchers on top of cases of medical stores. This meant that when the weather was wet, and it soon became very wet, we could sleep anywhere in the truck and did not have to bother about other shelter from the rain. I was usually out with a battery, and lived and ate with my own section, only joining the Officers' Mess when the whole regiment was stopped for several days in a village.

During most of April we were in the part of Central Burma that lies between Meiktila, the Irrawaddy and Allanmyo. The country was mostly low and undulating, often dry and rocky. On 24 April we reached Taungdwingyi, in latitude 20 degrees N. The soil was baked hard and the vegetation, except where there was irrigation, thorn and cactus. Large tracts of the country were irrigated, using dams, canals and lesser watercourses called 'distributories'. By this means the paddy fields could be flooded and during at least part of the dry season luxuriant vegetation grew in the villages that were near canals – great trees, banana groves, palms and proper grass. During the monsoon large areas were flooded. Houses were raised off the ground and every village had its pagodas, and often a *Pongyi Kyaung*, or combined school and small monastery.

We did not see many Burmese, and the pongyis we saw had a sullen look, but I did see a unit of Burmese guerrillas who were said to have been actively on our side. They carried an assortment of weapons: silver-plated pistols, Japanese swords, shotguns, Jap rifles, crossbows, spears, sharpened bamboos, dahs and, said the padre, blowpipes. The only blowpipes I saw were those used by villagers to hunt frogs in roadside ditches; the pipes were ten feet long and made of bamboo, and the eighteen-inch arrows were barbed and feathered. The villagers shot the frogs that sunned themselves at the edges of ponds and strung the bodies on arrow shafts carried over the shoulder.

On 25 April we reached our destination about three in the afternoon. There I chose a place for my section and we dug three slit trenches and drank tea. Between four and six in the afternoon I held a sick parade. I ate near my truck and after sundown Richard Crookes, a new Padre, came over for a talk. He was a tall, lean man from Pembroke College, Cambridge, with personality and intelligence and a face like a curate. He was not long from home and he felt the heat. We were getting daily temperatures of over 110 degrees in the shade. We sat in the open under the moon sipping whisky until 2130 and were joined by the Battery Commander, Warren Bugler, who had just heard that he had been granted a month's home leave and wanted to celebrate. He was a leathery-faced well-built man, tanned, clean-shaven, with dark hair. He was very interested in the men's welfare and had a good way with them; he was quiet, observant, intelligent and perhaps a bit religious – a nice fellow.

At Taungdwingyi the battery had stopped for the night astride a road down which a south-bound Japanese convoy was expected. It arrived in the dark and drove blindly into the muzzles of the 25-pounders which were aimed to shoot straight up the middle of the road. The destruction at close range was such that there was no work for me.

We were halted one day by trouble on the road ahead. A 5.5 inch gun belonging to a Medium Regiment had had an accident. It was an accident to which these guns, the men told me, were prone. The gun was firing on some target miles away and a shell had exploded on leaving the muzzle – a 'premature' it was called. In action, when casualties were part of the day's work, men took things as they came, but when something like this happened they nursed a smouldering resentment against everything and everyone. One man had been badly hurt and after I had done what I could we sent him to the nearest Field Ambulance.

During the ten days to the end of April the batteries were a good deal in action in support of units that were clearing Japs from positions in the neighbourhood of the road and river. At night, as well as using the Dodge truck, we sheltered from the heavy rain in derelict houses and sometimes in roofless buildings over which we rigged tarpaulins. Heavy rainstorms had now begun.

We heard on the wireless of the triumphant advance of the Allies into Europe, but our men did not "enter beautiful little towns to be greeted by waving crowds of laughing girls with baskets of fruit and bouquets of brightly coloured flowers". Instead, at the beginning of May, they drove or trudged all day in rain and came at the end to empty villages.

On 4 May we came through Prome in pouring rain; it was a desolate, derelict and empty town, fallen to ruin and overgrown with weeds. North of Prome the road ran for long distances by the Irrawaddy and through squalls of rain we had glimpses of great sheets of water with here and there what looked like islands. Prome was distinguished by an enormous brick and plaster Buddha. I measured the fingers as about eight feet long. That night we reached Shwedaung and my people settled into a tin-roofed teak house that was in good condition. The adjutant put up a sign – 'Bedside Manor'.

Driving south over a bit of open country on 8 May, I came across one of our 15-cwt trucks halted, with a group of men gathered round the back listening to a wireless that was tuned to the BBC Overseas and Forces Programme. The European war was over. A surrender had been signed at some place called Lüneberg Heath. Ten days back we had been overjoyed to hear a rumour that something like this was going to happen; now we were rather indifferent about it. What, we wondered, were the chances of being relieved by troops from home? That was all; we had no great feeling about the end of Nazi Germany.

The Regiment settled at Shwedaung for a week while individual batteries or troops of guns went out to villages and across the Irrawaddy in support of units mopping up Japs to the west of the river and in the Pegu Yomas.

There was very little work at Shwedaung. Sick parades were small; I toured the camp each day to get to know people and to look at the kitchens, water supply and latrines; and from time to time I visited medical units like the nearest Field Ambulance. Occasionally I had calls that were out of the ordinary. I made friends with a young girl called Ma Kyia; she had had her ears pierced, and her father brought her to me because the small wounds were septic and messy, and spoiled her appearance. When cured and beautiful again she rewarded me by coming in her best clothes with jasmine flowers arranged like a tiara in her hair, bringing a basket of ripe mangoes.

Later her uncle took to sitting with me and as he had a bit of

English I began to learn a few words of Burmese. I discovered that in Burma you changed your name with your age. For instance Ma Kyia at 40 would be called Ta Kyia and her uncle, now called Maung Mia Ten, in middle age would be Ko Mia Ten and in old age U Mia Ten. All this I picked up slowly and it was some time before I realized that the prefixes like Maung and U corresponded to words of address like 'brother' and 'old man'. I had taken to wearing a lungyi about my middle and while we were talking one evening Ma Kyia came along and with a smirk pointed at my waist and said something to her uncle; unwittingly, I had knotted the lungyi round my waist with a knot used only by women and this had to be adjusted. I found pronunciation difficult and made ridiculous mistakes like suggesting that we make a trip on the Irrawaddy in a bullock cart: to the untaught ear the words for boat and bullock-cart were very much alike. Ma Kyia's love for me lasted until she found that my driver, Schlaepfer, had an inexhaustible supply of chocolate.

I began about then to give talks on VD to gatherings of BORs, a battery at a time. I had never felt at home lecturing and was pleasantly surprised to find how easy it was to talk about a subject you knew, and in which the audience was deeply interested. I had extended my repertoire to include the other subject in which they were all deeply interested – sex. 'Audience participation' and 'emotional involvement' were such that during a talk one or two of the biggest and toughest-looking regularly passed out in a faint: it was gratifying to be so appreciated.

On 25 May I summoned the 15-cwt after lunch and with Schlaepfer and Lawrence went off to vaccinate the men of a battery about ten miles away. The countryside around was flat at first, mostly paddy, with here and there a clump of palms and other trees marking a village. After a few miles we reached low hills, about 200 feet high, mere undulations in the generally flat plain; there were more trees and freshly sprouting paddy with a delicate green of its own. Soon we came to a small village that the war had not touched. The bashas were tidy, the people looked leisurely and well-fed and there was a small bazaar. An appetizing smell of curry was in the air and we saw livestock on the road – ducks, chickens, cows, a sow with piglets, sleek fat goats and two well-groomed horses. Behind the village, on a wooded hill, was the best-kept pagoda I had seen. It was shapely, about 80 feet high, tapering; the gold paint was fresh and there were none of the flashes and squiggles of paint that cheapened the look of many pagodas. At the village we left the road and took a track south-west through thickets of bamboo and over streams to more open country. In the far distance was a bluish range of hills beyond which lay the Bay of Bengal.

As we bumped along the track or squelched through streams I saw a variety of birds that made up for a comparative lack of them in the last few weeks. Ankle-deep in water were snowy white egrets with black bills and legs. They stood about two and a half feet high, had white crests and moved very delicately. With them were pond herons or paddy birds. They had white wings, grey backs and rusty heads and necks. Their bills were a faint light blue and they stood about 18 inches high. Another small heron was with them, the night heron, black, grey and white. Drongos and bulbuls were common in bushes by the track; the drongo looked like a blackbird with a forked tail. We reached the village where the guns were; I did my vaccinations; we had a mug of coffee each and at 1630 started back. The sun was behind us and in that rainy season the air was clear, showing the distant trees in sharp relief.

The village we had come through in the afternoon was now awake – the golden pagoda was bright in the setting sun, the villagers were by the wells or strolling under the trees. On the road we met two young priests with shaven heads; they stood upright and had a calm and dignified look; they wore the saffron robes of their class and one of them carried an open parasol. They were about 18 years old and were probably novices. Farther along the road we passed a well. A young woman clad only in a lungyi stood beside it pouring water from a bucket over her body. She had very black hair and light brown skin and was slim and good-looking. All along the way, now that it was evening, we passed Burmese either on foot or in bullock carts. They were active only in the mornings and evenings. Shwedaung, when we reached it, was hotter than any place we had been during the day, and drier, whiter and dustier.

I took off my clothes at sunset, stood on the verandah and poured cold water over myself using half an old coconut shell as a ladle. I dried my hair and left my body wet. I wrapped a towel round my waist and sat on the bed. I had one bottle of beer left from my month's ration. A day like this was like an issue of fresh pineapples in a ration of bully beef and biscuits.

By 31 May the sun was passing to the north of us at noon. The coolest hour of the day was just after dawn, about 0645, when 80 degrees felt cool and refreshing. We moved south to Letpadan and west from the main Rangoon road to the quiet village of Sitkwin where for the next three months the regiment was to rest.

Chapter 13

Sitkwin

SITKWIN WAS ABOUT two miles west of the main road from Prome to Letpadan, Tharrawaddy and Rangoon. The regiment settled in towards the end of the first week in June. The Japanese had by now been cleared from our part of Burma although there may have been some stragglers in the Arakan Yomas to the west of the Irrawaddy. The regiment was no longer in action and for the next three months we were busy with little more than maintenance, repair work, training and recreation.

Sitkwin had a pleasant broad tree-lined main street, bordered by fine houses in their own gardens; they had a framework of teak and walls of bamboo matting. Similar houses lined the side streets. All the houses were raised off the ground and were approached by a few steps. Many of the roofs were of corrugated iron, necessary in the heavy rains. There was a school run by pongyis or monks, and a Police Station which consisted of little more than an office and a rudimentary lock-up. The pongyis occupied a large house which I never visited. There were a number of pagodas on the outskirts.

The village had not been much damaged by war, the houses for the most part were in good condition and, although we commandeered some of them and had our gun parks on land all round, the inhabitants greeted us civilly, the Burmese, particularly the pongyis, with aloofness, and the Karens, Chinese and Indians in friendly fashion. It was delightful to see the Burmese in the cool of morning and evening sauntering up and down the streets clad in the long skirts and small blouses or coats of the country, the women wearing sandals and wide-brimmed hats, carrying parasols and smoking cheroots, usually of the fat white sort. The "whacking white cheroots" were made of a maize leaf rolled into a cylinder six inches long and an inch in diameter, filled with tobacco. The tightly rolled end was put in the mouth and the other end closed with a twist or tie. The men wore bright coloured silks on their heads and the women, bare-headed, wore their hair in a bun, usually with a comb in it. As well as the skirt or lungyi women wore a little jacket or *engyi* that buttoned right across the front; their underwear consisted of a long embroidered cotton or linen vest with shoulder straps.

Regimental Headquarters occupied one pleasant house and I commandeered another across the road for the medical staff and sick bay. I allocated a spacious room on the ground floor as the MI room where I could see patients; two other rooms on the same floor served as medical store and sick bay. My staff and I lived on the first floor, where there were three rooms. Lawrence and two others slept in one, Richard Crookes the padre had a room to himself where he could see people in private, and I shared the third with John Palmer, Regimental Intelligence Officer. It was a fine room with teak floors on which we spread grass mats. There were comfortable bamboo beds, a remarkable dressing table with drawers and full-length mirrors, and several earthenware pots which someone had filled with flowers. The walls were of woven bamboo. The windows could be closed with flaps made either of woven bamboo or of bamboo strips. Through the windows we saw only foliage: mango trees, palms and a striking tree with scarlet-orange flowers, known to us as Flame of the Forest, which we often admired as we drove on the country roads. Downstairs in a corner of the MI room was a water filter consisting of two earthenware pots one above the other. The upper pot held a layer of coarse sand through which the water dripped into the lower pot and gave us cool clear water at all times. The garden before the house was about 15 yards square and had growing in it jackfruit, lime, mango, betel nut, betel leaf, banana, papaya and tamarind, and a *neem* tree – you could use the leaves of the *neem* to keep off fleas and bed-bugs, and the frayed ends of its twigs made a good toothbrush. There were also in the garden a hairy black pig and some fowls, which fluttered wildly when alarmed.

We had hardly moved in on the first night when a man and a girl were brought to me with burns on hands and feet, and I guessed that I should soon have a civilian practice. I enjoyed attending to the Burmese: they did not come unless they had something definite wrong with them, like a cut or a boil or a burn. Sitkwin bore one or two scars of war and it was because of this that I had my next patient from the village. Near the outskirts was a large store of rice which at some time had been set on fire, either by the retreating Japanese or accidentally by our gunfire. Before our arrival a small Indian boy playing in the neighbourhood had been dared to jump into the rice which, though it looked harmless, was still smouldering below the surface. He had second degree burns a week old and his blistered feet were septic. After I cut away the dead stuff and cleaned him up he healed very well, and my modest success and willingness to help established trust; a visit from the boy's parents to bring a few gifts gradually grew into a custom of bringing sick people to see me every day. There were fevers, wounds and infections, and common diseases that I could recognize and treat; there were also a great number of complainants whose illnesses, even when real, I had no means of diagnosing.

I had to find some way of communicating with my patients; the problem solved itself when I found that one of the idle spectators in my MI room lived across the road. He was Maung Hla who spoke English and was willing to interpret; he was also always ready to take me to other villages if someone there was sick, and at his house he would put up anyone from a distant village who needed to see me daily. He was very good with children and had two of his own. He was naturally inquisitive but if his do-gooding had any ulterior motive I never saw it. He was a good sort, glad to be of help. Before the war he had been a clerk in the oil wells at Chauk, near Yenangyaung, and after I left Burma I had a letter from him to say that he had got a job with the Government Civil Affairs Organization.

Late one night Maung Hla took me to an Indian woman in labour. During two years in the army I had become used to fevers and wounds of all kinds, but childbirth was something that had not come my way and it was with very little confidence that I went in the dark to a small shack on the outskirts of the village. There was a midwife in Sitkwin and I found her sleeping under the patient's roof. Her own child suffered from impetigo and was also there, a bearer of infection, whom I was not at all pleased to see; fortunately he was already being treated by Bombardier Lawrence and was painted all over with the violet antiseptic that we used. As far as I could tell the labour was going well, except that the mother was suffering from exhaustion; thinking that after a good rest she would get on and finish the job by herself, I gave her a dose of some medicine we used to calm the nerves of soldiers who were over-excited and went back to my bed wondering what on earth to do if things went badly next day. Before dawn I was called again and to my surprise was handed a note which read,

> 'June 19th, '45. Dear Doctor, Thanks very much. It is with great joy that I inform you a boy is delivered exactly at 2 o'clock a.m. The boy and the mother are both in pink of condition. Everybody in the household render their heartfelt thanks to you.
> Faithfully yours,
> R. Kahn.'

More children were born in the village and as time went on I found that nature worked wonders and that masterly inactivity worked wonders too – for my reputation.

A few days later two pretty girls presented themselves at the MI room; they had done some nursing and were willing to act as nurses and interpreters and would happily conduct me to other parts of Sitkwin to see patients too sick to be brought to me. I engaged them on the spot and never regretted it, but my excursions with them were sometimes misunderstood by officers at RHQ and I became the object of slightly envious raillery.

The gunners, as was the way with British soldiers, soon had friends in every part of the village and did a brisk trade in bananas, chickens, mangoes and perhaps less innocent purchases. Even at Sitkwin all was not parasols and smiling faces, and behind many of the bamboo walls there were unfortunates desperately sick with neglected infections or untreatable illness.

Water for the regiment was brought from river or well in the regiment's water-cart, a small motor tanker on the back of which some humorist had stencilled, 'GUNGA DIN Mark II, 200 Gals'.

All our water, whether from the river or from the deep brick-lined village wells, however fresh and pure it might look, had to be treated before use; for in every Sitkwin back garden was a cesspit, an open brick-lined hole full of ordure seething with maggots, the breeding ground of flies and a perpetual headache for me.

Soon I had settled into a daily round which changed little while I was at Sitkwin. I would be up at 0530, join in PT for half an hour, and have a stand-up bath. After breakfast I did the men's sick parade and visited the batteries to talk with the Battery Commanders about anything that affected their men and concerned me. Between 0945 and 1030 I did a round of visits to housebound civilian patients who lived not too far away. Then, from 1100 for an hour and a half, I held a sick parade for civilians. I had many Burmese patients in the mornings and we were always short of the right drugs for them. The Burmese nurses did the dressings, for I did not want the BORs to have anything to grouse about if I could help it.

In the afternoon the rain came down steadily, fresh and cool. From 1400 to 1500 I went the round of the unit latrines. After that I was available to be called out to see new cases in the village: my Burmese teacher's nephew, aged 8, was sick with malaria, an old woman had a poisoned leg, a middle-aged woman had a benign growth in the womb, another had violent pains due to kidney stones; there was no end to it and by six o'clock I was ready for a bottle of beer.

Each day at 1600 a Burmese teacher who happened to own the house I had commandeered called to give the Padre, the IO and myself a language lesson. He was spotlessly dressed in shirt, lungyi and slippers. He had been a schoolmaster and because he under- stood our questions he was a better teacher than someone less intelligent would have been. He had a sense of humour – more, perhaps than was good for him, for after the end of the war he wrote to tell me he was in gaol, "because I made fun with the Police inspector". Richard and John Palmer and I would sit round on low chairs squeezing information out of him. I asked most of the ques- tions because I had already tried to pick up bits of the language and had a head start. I wrote in an exercise book my own phonetic version of what I was being taught and was able to pick up a certain amount of grammar while at the same time extending my vocab- ulary. I was delighted by the picturesqueness of the language: how fitting to say when you have a headache that your 'head bites' and to refer to malaria, in which the fever rises and falls like a bird in flight, as 'bird fever', and to call a common and apparently almost universal kind of venereal disease 'boy fever'.

With interpreters to help when I got into difficulty it was not long before I could question the villagers about their ordinary affairs and their complaints and tell them how to take their medicines. In social intercourse I had to be more careful. When pleased to meet someone it was customary to say "*Win tha de*" – my bowels feel warm, and not to say "*Win twa de*" – my bowels are running, apparently a common mistake. My range of grammar and vocabulary was limited to phrases regularly used between doctor and patient, a severe handicap at a tea party; after long search for an inoffensive topic the best I could do might be to start the conversation with a bright smile, saying airily, "I do not have a headache today".

The Burmese could be emotional and violent and I encountered extremes of gentle courtesy and hot-tempered physical assault. One morning a young man was brought with a head wound, a saucer-like depression in his skull, half the size of a tennis ball. When I asked how he had come by it he said, "My uncle hit me". "Why?" "Well, my bullock strayed into his garden and he lost his temper." Although the blow seemed for the time being to have cured the quarrel I had to send him to hospital.

My patients were of all races – Burmese, Indians, Chinese and Karens, many of whom were Christians and spoke English. The only people with whom I had very little to do were the young priests, the pongyis with shaven heads and saffron robes who seemed always aloof and perhaps hostile.

I was brought presents from time to time: cheroots, coconuts and especially bananas, of which I usually had a branch in one of our rooms, covered with a blanket to ripen the fruit. One day a child of eight whom I had been treating for a ragged and septic wound in the hand came to me in the middle of the BOR sick parade and, taking my hand, put in it a small bundle, saying very shyly, "*Chet-u yu la bi*, (I have brought eggs)".

The gunners gave me very little work. Officers and senior NCOs made sure that everyone took his daily suppressive Mepacrine tablet for malaria and in general they were a fit crowd of men. From time to time we went out into the country for a run of a few miles in which we all joined. It was only rarely that I had to attend to anything serious among the men or officers. One of those occasions was late at night when I was asked to see a new officer who had just joined the regiment. I found him lying covered with blankets, shivering violently and semi-delirious with high fever. He had a bad attack of benign tertian malaria and next day I told him he ought to be admitted to a Field Ambulance. He protested violently at this and as I had probably treated as many cases of malaria in the last year as anyone then in the Field Ambulance I consented to look after him where he was. Charlie Armour was red-haired and freckle-faced and looked about 17; before long he was as well as the rest of us. He had a good brain and would soon be going home to resume an interrupted Cambridge career reading geography. He had been trained in survey in the army and my first thought was that here was someone who might be persuaded to take some leave to explore in the mountains.

Only occasionally did the regimental work pile up so that I felt harassed: I had a lot of medical inspections to do and the CO was for a time very testy with a stiff neck; it cured itself after I had provided him with a masseuse from the village. We became good friends and I treasured some of his remarks: "It's not an officer's job to make himself popular, it's his job to make himself respected." He pulled my leg in a good-natured way about what he called my private practice, the size of the private income I derived from it and the benefits in kind: "The Doc had to be lifted again off that nurse to get him here in time for dinner". 'Happy' Apted, a prospective schoolmaster with glasses and curly hair, who replaced John Palmer as IO and shared my room, was the only person interested in what I really did in the village. Most were indifferent or made a joke.

The nearest I came to a disagreement with the CO was one day when he told me that he expected me to report to him any man with VD. I had just told the men that they could come to me about VD in confidence, and this put me in a difficulty. I told the CO that if he insisted I should first have to tell the men that I would be reporting those with VD, and until that was understood I could not do as he asked. He grunted and I heard no more about it.

While we were at Sitkwin a Professor La Bu, once principal of a college in Rangoon, came to talk to the regiment about Burma during the Japanese occupation. He was small, about 5ft 6ins, in height, and very slight, aged about 50. He had black hair with a few greyish flecks, light brown skin and a characteristically Burmese face. His hair was cropped short and he wore a dazzling white shirt, unbelievably white compared with our drab greens. It had no collar and was fastened at the neck with a silver stud. He wore a dark blue lungyi and over all a short grey collarless jacket of embroidered silk with cloth fastenings fashioned in elegant loops. The whole costume was smart and the impression he gave was of neatness and delicacy. He seemed fastidious and physically did not look robust. The only item in his dress which jarred was a pair of shiny black European shoes. I dined in the mess with him after he had given the men the talk about Burma and I was able to ask him a lot of questions. He liked to indulge in a sort of "I know English language" style of humour: "When the Japanese first came they talked of 'co-prosperity' but it soon became clear that the prosperity was for them and the 'co-operating' for us." I could imagine him living blandly with the Japanese, keeping his own counsel, betraying nothing. He told me with no change of expression, no stiffening of the body, no tremor in his voice, that the Japanese did to prisoners "things that make my blood boil". I did not ever know what he felt.

His worst experiences, it seemed, were being accused of hiding when he had gone behind a cactus to empty his bladder, and being mistaken for a Jap and almost shot by Americans near Myitkina. Neither experience seemed very terrible to his audience of seasoned gunners. He said that the Japs came with overtures of friendship, but that their behaviour deteriorated steadily during their stay in Burma. To him, their awfulness was due less to atrocities than to their lack of respect for Buddhism and for persons, and to the presence of the *Kempei tei* or Secret Police in Rangoon. Their chief offences in his eyes were walking into shrines with their boots on, bathing naked in the open, slapping the faces of Burmese officials and ordering priests to draw water for them. These were particularly odious offences, but fear, he said, was the worst thing of all and it was release from fear that made everyone happy at the moment of liberation.

He told me that the irrigation system in Burma as it was in 1945 was built by the British, but that before the British an earlier and more primitive form of irrigation was in use, of which he could give no details. The Burmese, he said, bury their dead, except for the pongyis, who are cremated. The pongyis he described as teachers who gave their lives to meditation and learning; they performed no ceremonies like burial or marriage but were invited as honoured men to be present on such occasions. Boys, who all attend the pongyi kyaungs, go through a novitiate of a few months or a year whether they are to be priests or not, and during that time they wear the saffron robes and carry begging bowls. I was in the mess the next night when the CO started to talk about La Bu, what a wretched fellow he was and what a rotten talk he had given. I said that I had rather liked him and, after waiting a moment, the CO said, "I thought he was a frightful wet," and the adjutant chipped in, "Yes, Sir, all Burmese are like that". It seemed odd that a man like the CO should crash through Burma and see so little to interest him by the way.

Yacoob, the Indian barber, came from the village to cut my hair; he told me that when the Japs came in 1942 his father had set out for India on foot. He had had no news of him, and when I offered to send a letter for him to his home in Bihar he was effusively grateful; he told me that all he wanted was to say that at Sitkwin all were well, and he produced a letter pathetic in its directness.

"Who is alive there? Did my father reach home? I am alive and well." Later he wrote more that went on for page after page of love, of the sadness of separation, and of the pain of having no news. I never knew if he had any answer.

On 22 June the Padre and I went to Rangoon by jeep. We left at 0930 and got there at 1400. In one place I drove the jeep into a paddy field and thought we were stuck for good. The approach to Rangoon was along bomb-cratered highways wide enough for two and sometimes four lanes of traffic. We saw the rubble of recent bombing and the bustle of a seaport that was by then the only supply line for a whole campaign. As we entered the city we passed through a wide park. To the east was a wooded hill and on top of it, above a forest of palms, the Schwe Dagon pagoda – golden, elegant, simple. We carried on into the town past endless sleazy bazaars, with displays of fruit, hardware, footgear and cotton cloth; we came to tramlines, streets pitted and torn by bombs, burnt-out houses, derelict offices, tumbledown warehouses. It was a town unkempt and battered. I strolled among crowds of Chinese in markets where the quality of everything was poor and the price high. I had my first sight of a ship as I walked in the Chinese market – the masts and funnels of a merchant steamer. After that nothing would do but a visit to the docks, where we saw ships at the quayside and at anchor out in Rangoon harbour. Local boats drifted past; each had three head of cattle in tow, swimming along behind. There was a great coming and going of launches and lighters, and a busy traffic of coolies, crates, cranes and sailors. I came away with two memories, the Schwe Dagon pagoda and the waterfront; otherwise Rangoon was disappointing.

Rosita, one of the nurses, a quiet girl with a sense of humour, took a few of us to a Karen Christian service; it was a mixture of the ridiculous and the moving. Four girls sang a hymn in broken English about 'My lovely Saviour being yours' or something of the sort. They sang in four parts and though the voices were not good they were in tune and the whole performance reminded me of a village chapel service at home. The Buddhist Burmans could be charming in a thoroughly worldly way that I understood but these Christian Karens had a strange air of mildness and purity. The Karen language sounded musical and soft and I was happy to listen to the voice of an old man praying, though I had no idea what he was saying.

Richard preached a sermon in flowery English, beginning, "My dear friends. It is with a deep sense, I say it again, with a deep sense . . ." It occurred to me that none of this would be literally translated into Burmese or Karen but into vivid speech in which "I understand" was "My ear turns round" and "Listen" was "Prick up your ears". Speech in which your bowels "grew small" when you were sorry and "glowed" when you were happy. As I listened to the old Karen translating Richard's sermon I thought his way of speaking a delight to hear; he spoke softly yet strongly and the tone of his voice rose and fell.

Talk in the Regiment was often of the end of the war. The General Election of 1945 had come and gone. My feeling about it was that I did not care who got in so long as they left me alone to live my own life in my own way. I thought the Conservatives more likely to do that. Most people in SEAC just did not vote. About one third voted by proxy, a handful actually sent in their votes, and the rest said, "What the hell?"

Many of the older men were being repatriated; the Government had suddenly, before the Election, shortened by four months the period of service needed in the Far East to qualify for repat, and "Roll on Repat" had become a refrain. But the war was not over for us, and the Generals were upset at losing senior men.

I was unsettled in my own mind about my own future. I did not want to rush home to doctor, and I wondered about being demobilized where I was, in order to travel in the mountains. Like many young men, I no longer fancied a steady job at home. When the postwar Labour government was elected there was a great deal of talk among doctors about the future of medicine at home, and I had an idea that to work in a state-run medical service in a socialist Britain might not be what I wanted at all. My prejudice against a state-run service was strengthened by an encounter with the CO of the British Military Hospital in Rangoon. I had in the regiment a young officer with skin trouble; he had been treated by a skin specialist somewhere else but the trouble recurred, and I took him to the hospital for advice. I could not find any 'skin man' to whom I could explain the circumstances, so I went along to the CO of the hospital, a full colonel, RAMC. I expected, as a visiting doctor, to be treated as an equal, in the way that John Wakeford and the ADMS of 20th Division, and also my CO in the gunners treated me. I put it to him, perhaps too forthrightly, that I had brought an officer who had been seen by a specialist elsewhere and that, as our regiment was due to move, I did not want to leave him until I knew that he would be in good hands. I had taken a dislike to the set-up at the hospital and I unwisely added for good measure that he would be better off with me and in his own unit than if he were to be pushed about from pillar to post. The Colonel was furious and shouted at me to put the patient in a ward and clear out of his hospital. I left at once but took the patient with me. I was very glad later that I had done so: he was much happier to be staying with the regiment and very soon his skin condition began to heal.

The experience left me with a vision of what the General Practitioner might feel when a bureaucratic hospital official was rude to him. In private medicine the specialist who wished to succeed had to be careful how he addressed the GPs who brought

167

him his bread and butter, but the position of the GP *vis à vis* the hospital might be less happy under the state.

At the end of June one of our men was found in a compromising position with the daughter of the local Chief of Police at her home. The Regimental Police rounded up the girls at Sitkwin available for sex and next morning we sent them off to the Field Ambulance at Letpadan to be examined and, if necessary, treated. Perhaps they knew what it was all about but they certainly looked as if they were off for a jolly day at the seaside as we packed them into the back of a 15 cwt truck and waved them away, a gaily-dressed laughing bunch of scamps.

On 14 July a message came to say that Captain R.C. Evans was granted 16 days' leave at leave station. It meant for me a fortnight's trek in the Himalayas and I decided to go to Ranikhet.

Chapter 14

Kumaon and Saigon

ONCE AGAIN I had neither time nor opportunity to find a companion and I decided to rely on finding a porter at Ranikhet. I collected what kit I had that was suitable for the mountains and Richard drove me to Rangoon in his jeep. I flew first to Chittagong and then on to Calcutta where I boarded the Frontier Mail, changing to the narrow gauge for Bareilly and the railhead at Kathgodan. Finally a lorry took me up the last 6,000 feet to Ranikhet. For the next two weeks I wandered freely in the foothills of the Kumaon Himalaya at the foot of Nanda Ghunti and Trisul.

Back in Ranikhet I heard on the wireless that a new kind of bomb had been dropped on Japan and that Russia had seized the moment to declare war. By the time I reached Calcutta the second atomic bomb had been dropped and there were rumours that Japan had capitulated. Calcutta was in uproar. As I sipped my drink in the foyer of the Grand a party of sailors came shouting up the wide front steps; they led a horse and ghari to the bar for a pint which they forced down the animal's throat. The sailors were more minded to celebrate than anyone and that night at a film show they marched across the front of the auditorium singing Rule Britannia.

Bill Haden from 111 Anti-Tank Regiment was at The Grand, on his way home for demob, and we started to talk about plans for after the army. I had a living to earn but no dependants; I thought that a specialist training in surgery would be the obvious thing to go for, especially as I liked working with my hands. Bill was going back to being a schoolmaster. He asked me how I had spent my leave and I told him all about it, recalling my contentment with the shepherds of Nanda Ghunti. I told him that what I really wanted to do was to find some blank on a mountain map and fill it in. There could not be many blanks left and those were likely to be politically inaccessible. Nor did I know any of the right people. It would be some time before I was out of the army and I thought I had better use the time making inquiries. I wondered if my ADMS might help me approach the Royal Geographical Society and later he did. As I was in Calcutta I visited the Government Map Depot and talked to a major in the Survey of India. He was very helpful and explained that much of the Himalaya was still unexplored, especially to the east in the direction of Bhutan and Yunnan, an inhospitable region full of unrest, where the opium poppy grew and the stranger was unwelcome. I confirmed much of this in the next year, during which I pursued officials in the civil administration at Singapore and was given up-to-date and highly discouraging advice.

Bill and I cast back to our time together on the Irrawaddy bridgehead; I asked him what had given him equanimity in battle, reminding him that he had once told me that only an acceptance that death was certain had helped him. But I did not think one could reason about those things. Some men just were more placid under strain than others; Bill was one of them.

The final news of the Jap surrender came on 15 August. When the speech was relayed to us the words did not sound like those of a people that has been thoroughly beaten and was surrendering unconditionally. We felt as we listened that, if Japan got away with supposing that they had reached some sort of accommodation with us, then half our effort was thrown away. We did not like it.

Four days later I was in a lift at The Grand when a tall, athletic-looking man with a colonel's red tabs squeezed in by me. He was somehow familiar and we recognized each other at the same moment; it was John Wakeford and we arranged to meet for coffee next morning. I was very happy to see him again. I never had another CO I liked so much. He was still using a cigarette holder and tapping his cigarettes on a silver case before lighting them. We talked for a long time about the past and the future. He suggested that I might later feel like going to live in Rhodesia and told me to think over the possibility of a job with a mining company for which he worked; it was, he said, a big, rich company which ran its own hospitals and had its own medical services for employees. I told him my vague plans and he said that I should consider the offer of a surgical job with him after I had taken the Fellowship.

A few minutes after we parted a voice on the hotel tannoy announced that MOs and nurses bound for Rangoon could go that day by sea, and before six o'clock in the evening I was aboard ship.

When the two atom bombs had been dropped and notice of capitulation had come from Tokyo some of us thought that all was now over and that we could go home. We soon found that we were mistaken. For one thing the Japs did not seem to understand the terms of surrender and tried to treat unconditional surrender as a sort of honourable truce. In the vast area to the east and south of Burma the Japs were under arms; and in Indo-China, Malaya and elsewhere thousands of British, Indian, French, Dutch, and American POWs languished under atrocious conditions, many of them at the point of death. Those countries were also infested with Nationalists and Communists who had seen in the dispossession of the colonial powers by the Japanese and in the subsequent defeat of the Japanese a unique chance to seize power themselves. The prisoners of war had to be rescued, the Japanese had to be disarmed and sent home, and someone had to keep law and order while decisions were made about the future of the old colonies. The 20th Indian Division had been earmarked, though we did not know it, to take part after the fall of Burma in Operation Zipper, the invasion of Malaya; now we were called instead to occupy the southern part of French Indo-China, once known as Cochin-China and centred on Saigon. By mid-September General Gracey and advance elements of the Division had already flown to French Indo-China by way of Bangkok. The rest of us followed in more leisurely fashion by sea.

The dark and in the end disastrous story of French rule in Indo-China began at the end of the eighteenth century and continued into the twentieth. Indo-China was once regarded by France as her proudest colonial possession and included within its boundaries what were then known as Tonkin, Annam, Cochin-China and Cambodia, as well as part of Laos.

After the fall of France in 1940 the French colonial government, sympathetic to Vichy, was cut off from Europe and did not seriously resist when the Japanese entered Hanoi. The Japs gradually moved south and set up their 'Supreme Headquarters, South-East Asia' at Saigon, under Count Terauchi. It was from there that they directed the war in Malaya, Burma and the East Indies. Although there were pockets of resistance to the Japanese among Frenchmen up and down Indo-China a state of 'live and let live' existed in Saigon until March, 1945. Then, when the Japanese faced defeat in Burma, an Allied invasion of Indo-China from the west through Thailand became a possibility; the Japanese could not afford to have remnants of a western colonial power impeding defence against such an invasion, and many of the French were imprisoned, killed or driven into southern China.

Long before the Japanese were established in Hanoi or Saigon there had been two other movements afoot in Indo-China: Nationalism and Communism. The communist movement was inspired by Ho Chi Min who at that time had American support, in particular the support of the OSS. Roosevelt was unsympathetic to the colonial enterprises of the western powers and had no wish to see France re-established in Indo-China. Ho Chi Min, a man of outstanding ability as a political manoeuvrer, was in the confidence of the Americans and established throughout the country a network of communist cells. As late as 1945 there were still pockets of French resistance in remote places, beset by the Japanese and trying desperately to hold out, in need of food and ammunition; The Americans gave them no help, a bizarre state of affairs in view of the later American involvement in Indo-China.

While we waited in Rangoon for MacArthur's formal acceptance of Japanese surrender, Ho's communist Annamites gained power in Saigon, and when we arrived the city was a mess of warring factions: Vichy French, French who had been trying to organize resistance to the Japanese, armed and disciplined Japanese, other Japanese who thought that by going over to the Communists they might benefit themselves in some way, genuinely and innocently nationalist Annamites and lastly the communist Annamites under Ho, destined after many years of war to oust the French and Americans and take over what was left of the country, giving their leader's name – 'Ho Chi Minh City' – to Saigon.

At the end of September the Regiment, with Indian and Gurkha troops of the Division, boarded a comfortable old passenger boat of the B & I Steam Navigation Company, the *Rajuna*. As we steamed out of Rangoon I saw the *Ranchi* anchored in the river;

the hole in her side had been patched and the sight of her reminded me of our dismal time in Egypt. Life on the *Rajuna* was like being on a pleasure cruise. We idled on the deck waiting for the next meal, talked, basked in the sun, and got to know some nurses who were going our way. On 4 October we passed Singapore; the buildings along the sea front were tall and white, the sea clear and green and the only disturbance on the mirror-like surface was made by flying fish that came out to skim the water for fifty yards on either bow. A few hours later we were heading north into the South China Sea where the sea was a darker blue and there was a scattering of white horses. Merely to be free from regimental duties was a contentment and we did not bother with ship-board games or occupy our evenings dancing.

Dizzy Dale came to see me one day and said that I ought to go in for psychology. When I asked why he said, "Well, you've got a reputation for summing people up. Pete Furlonger was saying that he'd been to see you the other day and felt as if you were looking right through him and knew exactly what he was thinking." I had heard other people say the same thing; there must have been some kind of special look that came on my face when my mind was an absolute blank; whatever the cause, it could be very useful.

During intervals between meals Charlie Armour and I chatted up the ship's officers and were given lessons in the use of the sextant. I tried to interest him in the eastern Himalayas but he told me that when he went home he must think of a career and perhaps get married. When he asked for advice about marrying I could only reflect that I was a very unsuitable person to give it. All I could do was to outline the likely consequences and he remarked obscurely, "Ah yes, it is better to be bold than always to be sorry."

Now and then, remembering my leave, visions returned to me of the white ice and grey rock of Nanda Ghunti and Trisul against blue sky, framed in a wooden window and balanced by brown faces with slanting eyes and shaggy hair. I wrote letters to the Survey of India about the eastern Himalaya and wondered if I could get three months' leave there before going home. At the same time I questioned a surgeon who happened to be on the ship about how long it would take to work for the Fellowship examination of the Royal College of Surgeons. I decided that by the time I was 32 I might with luck be a Fellow of the College and also have behind me some experience of mountain exploration.

Arrival at Saigon was marked by a sudden change from the dreamlike atmosphere of a cruise to the realities of life on land. We disembarked and marched through the town past groups of Annamites, Chinese, Japanese and French; there was a desultory cheer and someone clapped half-heartedly.

The situation at Saigon was confused. The Division was expected to repatriate prisoners of war, disarm the Japanese and maintain law and order until the French should return in sufficient force to take over the country. This they were not expected to do before late November or early December and we were in the awkward position of maintaining western colonial rule over a nationalist native population with troops who were themselves Asiatics and who were either self-governing like the Gurkhas or, like the Indians, had been promised self-rule in the near future. The disarming of the Japanese was postponed and under our orders they shared in the protection of Saigon. Most of them helped us but there were those who still refused to recognize the surrender of Japan and joined the Annamites (Vietminh). The sphere of influence of the Division was limited to Saigon city and a small area near it. Had this not been so the job would have been impossible.

We settled down to two and a half months of cantonment life interrupted by occasional outings to train the gunners or to give artillery support to Allied troops. Saigon seemed civilized; the houses on each side of the wide avenues were well built and there were no filthy bazaars in the main streets, which were lined with trees and were shady, breezy and cool; the contrast with Rangoon delighted us. Our quarters were in the large colonial artillery barracks by the racecourse. It was a splendid building, spacious and shady with thick walls and wide verandahs. Armed Japanese were to be seen everywhere about the town and when we went abroad we went armed and never alone. We ate our dinner on the first night by lamplight because the Saigon power station had been put out of action by saboteurs; from then on the Regiment's own generators were rigged up to light the barracks. After dinner short bursts of rifle, Sten gun and LMG fire reminded us of nights in Burma, and some wished that those times were not over. I had visited the Field Ambulance and seen the body of one of our young officers, and I did not feel as they did. During that first night I was called to see a sick sergeant-major and noticed that on the outskirts of the city the sporadic small-arms fire went on all night.

I slept in a bungalow outside the gates. From my bed I could see the sun rise over the huge Saigon racecourse. I shared the place with Charlie Armour, Richard Crookes, the Padre and Sidney Woodruffe, who had once been a policeman in Southampton. It was cool in October but by November it was hot and sweaty, hotter than anywhere I had been at that time of year.

I had quarters fitted out as MI room, sick bay, storeroom and accommodation for the medical staff in the main barracks over the road. Bombardier Lang had gone back home and had been replaced by Bombardier Cooke, a tall Londoner with a long gloomy face and a passion for breeding and racing greyhounds. He had once been a porter at Guy's Hospital and was good at my kind of practical work, planning our accommodation and setting out my instruments. For cleaning and general donkey-work we had a Korean prisoner, a big flat-faced rather unpleasant-looking brute of a man whom Cooke treated with good-humoured astonishment: "Cor, yer are a 'orrible little bugger, aren't yer. 'Ere, 'ave a fag."

After the morning sick parade I did another for the Korean prisoners who worked for the regiment. They were a sullen, dull crowd, vicious-looking, short and powerfully built.

After lunch I might go into town, driving a jeep and being confused at first by the small roundabouts and the anti-clockwise circulation of traffic. It was delightful to hear the voices of well-turned-out women speaking French and to find the shops amazingly stocked with goods of quality. My schoolboy French was not much use but knowing that we were 'abroad' I would often by instinct break into Hindustani or Welsh, both equally embarrassing and in Saigon equally useless. In the evenings we often went into the town for entertainment; when the pianist Solomon came to Saigon I went to hear him every night. On the last night he played Bach Preludes and Fugues, a Haydn Sonata and some Beethoven – an enchanting break in the pattern of our lives.

I was kept busy with routine jobs as MO to the regiment and was not doing much to fit myself for a life of exploration. I began to feel that my life at Saigon was a dead end; one Saturday I took the morning off and made a plane table survey of Saigon race-course. All the necessary instruments were available and the result, though on a small scale, was accurate and raised my spirits. I planned with my usual optimism to take leave at home in '46/47 and return to India to take my discharge there, and visit south-west China. While in Burma I had saved about £600; it was in a Bombay bank and I felt that I had all the money I should ever want in the world.

About that time I heard that an expedition to Mount Everest was being planned. I felt far away and out of touch but wondered if I could get on it as the doctor. My only qualification was experience as an RMO and some knowledge of Urdu. My mountaineering ability would be surpassed by others. I did nothing about applying.

A Frenchman found me a Chinese teacher. Mr Wong was a shopkeeper cum schoolmaster, a small man who came secretly for an hour every afternoon on a bicycle. He was frightened all the time because the Annamites sometimes murdered Chinese who associated with Europeans. I paid him well but I was never sure that he would pluck up courage to come again. I liked him and we were very much at ease together. When he had been coming for some time we started playing chess – Chinese style. He taught me that you played on the lines, not in the squares; and the moves and the names of the pieces were different from those I knew. The King and Queen were the Emperor and Prime Minister, the moves of the Emperor were restricted to his Palace grounds, and so on. I made little progress, either with chess or the language, though I wrote everything down. One night we played Mahjong so late that he stayed because it was dangerous for him to be abroad after curfew. He retired to bed murmuring Chinese phrases, one of which he said came from Genghis Khan; it sounded like, "*Chen li: ru jum yeng*" – 'A thousand miles: no human smoke'. I liked the idea.

The Japs in Saigon had not at this time been disarmed and their officers and NCOs carried swords. They jumped to attention, bowed and saluted us punctiliously and obeyed orders. We had many of them scurrying around the barracks mending electric lights and so on, but their chief function was to give support in keeping order outside Saigon.

We were out of sympathy with the French who had gunboats, tanks and modern arms; the Annamites had spears, bows and arrows, and rifles and not much else. One of our officers who had been out with a 25-pounder in support of a French unit said that when the French attacked a village they approached the first hut and fired through the walls with an LMG. After spraying the hut they opened the door and emptied another magazine through it. They dared then to enter and if the inhabitants happened to be Chinese instead of Annamite they said, "*Excusez*" and went on to the next hut.

There was a Civilian Hospital where I sometimes sent men for treatment. It was near the French Police Station and the gunners begged me to return them to the regiment so that they could sleep in barracks; they said that at the hospital they were kept awake at night by the screams of Annamites undergoing interrogation. But the Annamites too had a bad reputation; they could be cruel, primitive and vindictive – it was just that we had expected the French to behave like civilized people.

Our forty or so officers dined in a central regimental mess. It was hardly possible to know everyone unless we went out together with a battery, or lived in the same house, or they happened to go sick. One officer, who moved in genteel Saigon society, to his surprise though not to mine picked up venereal disease and came to me to complain, "But she looked so respectable, and she didn't want to be paid or anything."

I had problems with the men catching venereal disease. Girls were available all over the place, and one man complained to me about a girl with whom he had been lying on the edge of the parade ground just outside the barracks: as well as her fee she had taken from him the rest of his money and his paybook or AB 64, a document more precious in the army than a passport.

I lectured them at intervals and arranged that in the MI room there would always be a tray of condoms to which they could help themselves without asking when they went into town. The sheaths disappeared at an alarming rate and I found that they were taken in handfuls and sent home by airmail to be ready for the man's repatriation, now for many of them not far away.

Batteries went out of Saigon several times during November and December and I accompanied them. Our small convoy bristled with weapons but as a rule all was quiet; I enjoyed the drives through new country but the men who had been out long with the Regiment were tiring of 'blank schemes', as the BORs called them. One lieutenant drove his guns into a paddy field, saying to his crews, "No. 1 here, No. 2 there" and so on. When he came back from attending to guns 3 and 4 he found No. 1 gun up to the axle in mud and asked the sergeant in charge, "Is your gun bogged Sergeant?"

"No Sir, I'm burying the bloody thing."

On one outing I had orders to visit a Jap Depot Medical Store to make an inventory and confiscate anything useful to our Service. I brought away whatever I thought it reasonable to bring, leaving them what I thought the minimum with which they could carry on. My finds included a beautiful Japanese microscope. I had to tell them, when they objected to what I was doing, that they could "put in a claim through the official channels". I felt a bit mean about it. I should have liked the microscope myself.

On another outing we did a 'practice shoot'. I drove several miles with the CO, Charles Armour and one or two others to a remote spot on a deserted hillside – our OP; from it we could over-look a small valley in which there were clumps of trees. I was instructed to pinpoint one of these clumps on the map, range on it and give orders to the twelve 25-pounders of the regiment to shoot at it simultaneously from five or six miles away. A shot at one spot by all the guns at once was known as a 'Mike Target' and was very thrilling for someone who had never fired anything bigger than a 12-bore shotgun or a hypodermic syringe. I spoke over the radio: "Mike Target, Mike Target, Mike Target. Map reference so-and-so, Height so many feet, Right ranging," and a 25-pounder shell would come screaming over for me to check the range and bearing. When I had the ranging shots bursting in the right place I would say, "Record as Mike Target 12," or whatever it was. Then came the climax – "Mike Target 12, Stand by" – "Mike Target 12 – FIRE!" and seconds later the salvo of shells whistled over our heads to burst around the chosen tree. The CO stood by, grinning like a satyr and pulling my leg every time I gave a wrong order. It may have been practice for the regiment but they were also out to give 'the Doc' a day's fun: I reckoned that in shells alone the taxpayer must have paid £5,000 for my little shoot.

On 9 December I returned, sunburned, dirty and tired, from a jaunt to a seaside resort near Cap St Jacques, or Cape Jakes as Bird my driver called it. We started on a Wednesday and came back on the Sunday – Pete Furlonger and another Battery Commander, Francis Casement, myself and two Troops from Pete's battery, complete with batmen, cooks, signallers, gun crews, junior officers, and guns. Owing to road blocks we took two days to cover the 80 miles to the coast, and on the first day we ran into an ambush in a place as quiet as a country lane in England, doves cooing, insects humming. Pete, with batman, driver and wireless operator was in the leading jeep, going up a small hill with jungle on each side of the track, when a machine gun opened up. Windscreens were smashed and several trucks had bullet holes but no one was touched except a Jap who happened to be coming towards us, walking harmlessly at the side of the road; he was killed. Pete sent a patrol through the bush and found a small abandoned trench in which were two crossbows and a few arrows. The crossbows were about 3 ft 6 ins across; the arrows were of bamboo with jagged barbs cut out near the business end; they were smeared with a treacly red liquid that looked like some sort of poison. They looked 'orrible, as Bird said. We had no more trouble and went on to a place just past the small town of Baria and camped in an empty house set back from the road. Drums beat at night and there was an uneasy atmosphere.

We moved on from Baria to Long Hai, clearing road blocks, to a house on a hilltop, fronting the sea, a rich man's villa, empty of furniture. In the distance, to the south, was Cap St Jacques. In the evening we tried to play poker and listen to the sound of the surf, but were distracted by the beating of drums. The men got jumpy too. About midnight someone fired a shot and then everyone began to see moving shapes. Shots were fired in the night at prowlers that were not there. A shameful episode.

We bathed next day in a big surf and in the afternoon went into the village of Long Hai for fresh fish, geese, ducks and pigs for which, to the astonishment of the villagers, we paid. I spent time with the fisherfolk; they were Chinese and had shallow boats 15 to 30 ft long with sweeps, a short mast and a small sail. Peter and I tried to get taken out for a sail but the boatmen said that the wind was too gusty. I thought the boats would probably only sail on a broad reach or with the wind aft. They fished with nets or a hand-line, baiting the hooks with scraps of fish. I watched one boat being fitted out for the night's fishing by three old Chinamen. As well as their fishing gear they had bottles of water, faggots of wood, a tray of sand for their fire, slow-burning rope's ends to light the fire perhaps, long fishing poles, bananas, a few vegetables, a cooking-pot and an anchor made of stones in a sack. I wished that we were going with them. A night out on the ocean in one of those boats would be something to remember. Later, from the shore, we watched the dozens of little lights bobbing up and down far out.

On the morning of our next to last day at Long Hai I was stung when I got up in the morning by a scorpion that was lurking in my swimming trunks. The sting was painful for a few hours but did no harm.

We went to Long Hai again on 12–14 December without being shot at, but next morning a signal came from the CO to say that 231 Battery, on its way to join us, had "run into heavy trouble"; we were told to return next day. That evening everyone was a bit jittery, BORs cleaning and oiling bits of Sten guns that had not seen daylight for weeks. We played Mahjong while the eerie drums beat on every side; they were probably part of an innocent Chinese celebration, but no one attended to the game. Pete was a good leader and at the evening Order Group gave all of us confi-dence. In Burma he had won a Military Cross and become adjutant. Then he was made Battery Commander and promoted to major. He was tall, 25–26 years old, with very fair hair, a bit thin on top. He was very good in a tight spot and when everyone was jittery he could produce the sort of rueful joke that cheers and makes what seems dark and gloomy lose its terrors.

We started in the morning at 0700. A 'tractor' went first, towing one of the guns so that if we had trouble on the road we could turn the gun and shoot over open sights at any obstruction. I rode in Pete's jeep; my waggon, A.3, was in the second half of the convoy. As it turned out we had a quiet run through, making contact by radio at halfway with the CO who had come out in a light plane and was overhead watching our progress until at Bien Hoa we were met by an escort of the Frontier Force Rifles.

The political situation in Indo-China was getting worse. We were disarming and imprisoning the Japanese and everyone knew that we and they would soon be leaving. Swords taken from the Japanese in Saigon were formally presented to officers in the Division and I attended a parade at which I was given a beautiful sword reputed to be 400 years old; it had belonged to a major. Pale young French troops with white knees were arriving by sea and we were told that the Annamites had offered temporarily to accept British rule rather than go back to being a French colony. Our ignorance, as junior officers, of what was going on was abysmal, and we had no idea that except for the neutral, or neuter as they were called, people like the Chinese, the 'Free Annam' party was communist all through, followers of Ho Chi Min. We did not like to think of the next few months there.

The ADMS came to tell me that 59th Field Ambulance was going to Borneo; would I like to take over a company that was going to Jesselton (Kota Kinabalu) in British North Borneo (Sabah)?: "It is a step to being 2nd in command; would you not like promotion?" I said, "Yes," though I knew I should miss the gunners. Mackenzie told me that Jackson had spoken to him too, and he advised me to take the chance; he promised to put in for me a recommendation for promotion, a promise that the new adjutant, Donald McCulloch, afterwards told me that he faithfully kept.

On Christmas Eve I transferred to the Field Ambulance. I should have fifty beds, and a staff of one Indian doctor, two BORs, and seventy IORs. As I had never been in a Field Ambulance in my life I should have a lot to learn. When we reached Jesselton the nearest other hospital would be at Labuan, an island 100 miles to the south; the rest of the Field Ambulance would be at Kuching, 600 miles farther. I looked forward to it. Two days later I had a farewell party with the regiment and toured Saigon until late at night when my friends set me down on the quayside, threatening to be back in the morning to see us sail.

Sailing with us on the SS *Aronda* were the 4th/2nd Gurkhas, whose CO was Lieutenant-Colonel Kitson and whose MO was a pleasant, humorous and intelligent Pathan called Alamgid Khan, which he laughingly translated as 'World-grappling Khan'. As we cast off, a Dogra pipe band on the quayside began to play 'Over the Sea to Skye', and 'Auld Lang Syne' and a few haunting tunes of their own.

Chapter 15

Borneo

MY LAST VIEW of French Indo-China was of 'Cape Jakes' and Long Hai where three weeks earlier we had been sea-bathing. We reached Jesselton in North Borneo on the last day of 1945.

The *Aronda* was another old B & I ship like the *Rajuna*, about 10,000 tons, with comfortable lounges and dining rooms, and 4-berth cabins. She did about 10 knots and before the war used to ply between Singapore, Rangoon, Hong Kong and Madras. Food always seemed good on a ship: fresh fish, fresh vegetables, freshly baked scones. We realized then how monotonous British rations on shore had become. The IOR rations were the same wherever we went but the IORs did not mind that; and besides, on the boat they suffered badly from sea-sickness.

We approached Borneo over a very calm deep blue sea. Our first sight of the island was of cloud, white cumulus cloud rising here and there along the coastline, heavy grey cloud covering long ranges of dull green dark hills inland. It lay in the hollows of the hills and curled over the crests of ridges. A mist base lay along the whole sea's edge. I read in a book once that the humidity in Borneo was high and that the temperature scarcely varied between 83 and 90 degrees Fahrenheit. From the sea it did not look like a country for which anyone would want to fight. We anchored off the small town and in the afternoon I went ashore to look at the site already chosen for us by the Australians whom we were to relieve. For three days we ferried baggage, men and vehicles to a small pier.

The Australians had taken over this part of Borneo after the Japanese surrender. They boxed up 6,000 or so Japs in a POW camp, put wire all round and saw to it that the camp was properly run. They also made the Japs build their own hospital and run it, under supervision. As senior MO, I was expected, in addition to being in charge of the Field Ambulance Company, to supervise medical arrangements for Allied troops and for the Japanese camp and hospital. The Australians were waiting to go home and were glad to see us. The Japs had treated the Australians cruelly in Borneo and the Australian division that we relieved filled their prisoners with stories of what our Gurkhas would do to them with their kukris when they arrived; in fact the Gurkhas began at once to fraternize and my first sight of the Japs and Gurkhas together was of big smiles and of cigarettes being handed round.

Much of Jesselton was a ramshackle shanty town built out over the sea on stilts; the single-storey wooden buildings stood on platforms several feet above water level. Under the platforms, which were reached by ladders, the inhabitants moored their *praus* or dugouts. In the main street were a number of white brick and plaster houses with red tin roofs; they gave the place a more solid look than the wooden shacks that made up the rest of the town. The only notable structure in the main street was a gallows; its framework was completely open, and a short ladder led to a platform with the trap through which the victim fell. The whole thing was well made and cared for, and the easy movement of the well-oiled mechanism suggested that it was for use and not for ostentation.

A little way inland was a small civil hospital built of brick and plaster and, farther inland and uphill, in bamboo bushes, the Japanese hospital which I came to know later. It was a lovely spot, the tropical island shore of romantic dreams, backed by low jungle-covered hills; not many miles away were the jagged summits of Kinabalu, nearly 14,000 feet high.

My camp was on a small promontory at the sea's edge under casuarina trees. The beach was generally clean and sandy except that between the camp and Jesselton the land was fronted extensively with mangrove swamp where small crabs scuttled about with a curious clattering noise. At high water when the moon was full the place was beautiful. It was cool at night and the surf was only 50 yards from my tent. Behind our camp was an inlet that filled at high water so that we seemed to be on an island. I went out on the first night to look round at the quiet tents on open sandy spaces under the tall trees and listen to the slow, regular sound of the breakers. The blue outline of Kinabalu was clear against the moonlit sky. I spoke to our Indian sentry who was eyeing the rising spring tide doubtfully; he wanted to know where it would stop. He had never lived by the sea and knew nothing of tides, let alone springs and neaps. The breakers were small, a line at the edge of the sand; the water beyond was calm inside a coral reef that was two or three miles out. I was tempted to sit up all night.

The force at Jesselton consisted only of one infantry battalion, the 4th/2nd Gurkhas, my Field Ambulance company and a few ancillary units, a REME detachment under Bill Darley, and an RE section under Guy Lathbury, both lieutenants.

The Lushais of the Field Ambulance were a good lot, robust, intelligent, grinning, mongoloid in appearance, with sturdy limbs. They had their own language, though most could also speak Urdu, and they had characteristic names: Nekhupa, Thansianga, Kapthianga and so on, quite unlike the Rams, Lals, Singhs and Mahomets of India. I had us photographed as a company. In our best bib and tucker we posed in the open, some sitting, some standing and others on benches at the back. Some of the men were smoking cigarettes and I said, or so I thought, to Dhanan Jai, "Jemadar Sahib, get them to put those cigarettes out". The order was given and when I next looked at them every man had a cigarette dangling from his lips. When my linguistic slip-up ('take out' for 'put away') had been corrected the photograph was taken, and the print shows us wooden, glassy-eyed, grimly unsmiling and as near as being at attention as was possible for the non-military.

All the garrison bathed in the sea, and one evening we had a bad invasion of large jellyfish with long thick tentacles. Many of the men, mine and the Gurkhas, had sting-marks on their arms and legs which lasted for days, dark marks where the tentacles had wound about their limbs. The stings did no lasting harm but were painful at the time.

In January there was daylight from 0600 to 1830, and twilight was very short. I shared a tent with two Australian doctors until they left for home. One of them told me how lying on his camp bed he noticed his companion suddenly freeze and by lamplight saw a snake appear at the neck of his pyjamas and slide to the ground. Some days later I was standing at night under the casuarinas when I felt something cold slide up my leg and immediately thought of that story; very slowly, trying not to move, I undid my waist belt to let my trousers fall, and out came a very small jumping frog. I ate now and then in the Gurkha mess or asked one or two of them to join me. The younger ones could talk nothing but Gurkhali and had no opinion of non-combatants like us, but I liked Kitson, the CO, and saw a good deal of the officers of my own age, Khan, the MO, Peter Sparkes, one of the company commanders with whom I later went up Kinabalu and Tom Wimbush, another company commander.

I dealt a lot with the Japs; many spoke English and I could always demand an interpreter. Some of them were in a shocking physical state; a typical so-called 'working party' was in rags, emaciated and lacking all energy; I sometimes felt ashamed to come in from a swim and walk by them sunburned and well fed. One man in twelve was in hospital and half of the others ought to have been there. I regularly went round their compounds and hospital, and inspected the sleeping huts, kitchens, wards and sanitary arrangements. It was hot and dry and there was no shade inside the barbed wire. One morning on my round I was given a Jap doll as a present. It was cleverly made of rags and wire by women prisoners and was presented to me by their head doctor. When I asked about food a Jap baker tried to explain how they improvised yeast; when I asked about dehydration a senior MO showed how they gave intravenous fluids by some ingenious arrangement in which coconut milk played a part; I could not but admire their ingenuity and discipline. They never complained to me, and when I entered a ward on my way round the hospital every nurse and orderly stood rigidly to attention. So did those patients who could stand; those who could not stand lay at attention on their pallets on the floor.

The senior Jap MOs wore leather knee boots and came everywhere with me, followed by juniors who sucked pencils and diligently made notes; the juniors, interpreters and ward staff wore wooden sandals. I found them embarrassingly anxious to please.

Protheroe, my Field Ambulance CO, came to see me at the end of January. He was horrified at the condition of the Japs and took away with him a lot of figures about them which I supplied for him to write a report; we hoped that SEAC might be moved to help them with basic supplies. Given those, they had the knowledge and resourcefulness to do everything else for themselves. In

Singapore, Mountbatten's staff was at the time trying captured Japs as war criminals; they seemed determined that Jap POWs should not be given even basic remedies for the diseases that most afflicted them. All I got as a result of the report that Protheroe sent in was a signal from SEAC:

"ON NO ACCOUNT WILL JAPANESE P.O.WS. BE GIVEN MEDICAL STORES FROM ALLIED SOURCES."

I did in fact supply the Jap doctors on the quiet with what I could spare of the essential stuff – Atebrin for malaria and Sulphaguanidine for the dysenteries.

In mid-January a Gurkha was brought to me because his jeep had overturned; he had a head wound that looked as if someone had begun a mastoid operation on him and left it unfinished: the ear and scalp partly torn away from the skull. After cleaning the wound and putting in a few stitches I left well alone and two days later I saw him driving his jeep with as much *attaque* as ever.

Two weeks later another Gurkha was brought in after another road accident. No other vehicle was involved in these accidents: the Gurkhas simply drove motors as if they were 'going over the top' all the time. That second man was deeply unconscious and showed no signs of coming round, so by radio I summoned a flying boat to take him to the Main Dressing Station at Brigade HQ, Labuan Island. The Sunderland, which looked enormous, arrived next morning and landed in the lagoon by Jesselton town. We paddled out with the unconscious Gurkha in a native *prau*, and lifted him in, thinking how out of place the slim dugout looked against the hull of the flying boat. I went to the flight deck to chat with the crew and thank them. Then I had breakfast ashore at the Gurkha mess with Peter Sparkes and we made plans for climbing Kinabalu. We decided to go on 5 February with 24 Gurkhas, my Jemadar and four Lushais.

As the crow flies Kinabalu is about 30 miles from the coast. Peter and I travelled the first 20 miles by car in a couple of hours and then walked for two days to reach Kaung, 2,000 feet above sea-level and ten miles west of the summit. The Gurkhas said that deer and pig were plentiful in the jungle, and Peter gave them the day off to go out on *shikar* with a local man who "could call up Barking

Deer"; they came back at nightfall with the tattered remains of a very small bird and we dined on bacon and eggs instead of venison.

From Kaung eight hours' walk in pouring rain took us over Tenampok pass, 5,000 feet, and down to Bundu Tuhan in a valley to the south. The natives were 'Dusuns', small cheery fellows wearing a loincloth or shorts and sometimes a vest made of bark; they went barefoot and carried *parangs*, long straight knives in wooden sheaths. They lived in *kampongs*, clusters of three or four huts. Several *kampongs* went to make up a village like Bundu Tuhan. The huts were raised on stilts and made of bamboo and leaves. Halfway along the side of a hut was a doorway reached by a short ladder.

We stopped at Bundu Tuhan a day, hoping for a break in the weather. The south ridge of the mountain was steep, about 45 degrees, and covered with soft, rich, soaking wet jungle; there were mosses, ferns, orchids, insect-catching pitcher plants, bamboo, rotting wood, and leeches and snakes. We climbed tree roots, forded streams and at about 12,000 feet reached rhododendron. We had left most of the party at Bundu. As well as local coolies, those who came with Peter and me were my jemadar Dhanan Jai, six of Peter's Gurkhas and three special locals; one of these was Daniel Hiw, half-Dusun, half-Chinese, who engaged and managed coolies for us. The other two were ragamuffins: Labuan, a self-styled 'guide', and Tongal, a 'priest', to make appropriate sacrifices to the spirit of the mountain at intervals on the way. The rites put the coolies in a good frame of mind and brought Labuan and Tongal a small income from the sale to us of eggs and fowls required for sacrifice.

Labuan was small and weedy, with pyorrhoea and bad teeth; I found later that on a steep jungle-covered hillside he could show any of us a clean pair of heels. The holy man was also lean and tough, but had a shifty look. We took 15 coolies and four 'slashers' who went ahead from Bundu with *parangs* to clear the track. The Gurkhas came for fun and carried only their personal equipment. They sang much of the time, cheerfully but monotonously; they seemed only to have three tunes and Peter said that the words for all the tunes were the same – "My girl's in the family way". They devoted their energies to Peter's comfort and mine, making beds and shelters for us and bringing us tea. We walked separately at first and in the rain and mist I veered off the inconspicuous track and was lost until Labuan missed me and came after me like a dog on the scent of a wounded bird. The path was steep; in places we climbed by notches cut in tree trunks, and from about 5,000 ft. to 7,000 ft. we were bothered by leeches. Labuan walked fast and lightly as a feather. We caught up the others and in the afternoon reached Kemberanga at 8,000 ft. in pouring rain.

Kemberanga, to which we had looked forward as though it were a comfortable hotel, was a dank clearing measuring 30 yards by 80 on a hillside too steep to lie across without rolling down. The slashers had put up leaf and bamboo shelters and lighted fires. We changed and draped our steaming wet clothes by the fires.

On our seventh day, 11 February, we started early in a drizzling rain which settled down almost at once to a downpour. The path was less steep and we climbed for three hours over boulders, moss, ferns, twisted trees and rhododendron to Paka cave at 10,000 ft. When we arrived I was shivering so much with cold that I could not even strike a match for a smoke. It had rained steadily for 48 hours and did not look like stopping. The Gurkhas lit two fires in the cave and slowly we came back to life. The roaring river outside was a series of waterfalls; everywhere was misty and damp, and we sat around for the rest of the day, hoping for improvement. The curtain of rain sometimes cleared enough to give us glimpses through cloud of the huge summit rocks described as 'Mediaeval Castles' in the only printed account of Kinabalu we had seen. The main Paka cave was formed by an overhanging boulder and was 8 feet deep by 15 wide by about 6 feet high. We closed the cave opening with leaves and raincoats hung on twigs. Outside there was steep jungle where the coolies found smaller caves in which to shelter. Only once did the cloud clear enough to give a glimpse of the distant sea thousands of feet below.

Peter and I lay by one fire while the Gurkhas at another fire used their kukris to slice vegetables into a pan. Beyond them was the leafy wall through which we could watch the rain. Tongal the priest did us no good with the weather and in addition turned out to be a spoilsport: he said that the mountain spirits would be displeased by shouting, singing and the sound of the *Sumputan*, a weird-looking wind instrument with pipes that made a pleasing low humming sound.

Above the cave steep jungle gave way to heathery trees and scrub that gave way in turn to steep slabs of fine grey rock speckled with black and criss-crossed with white quartzy bands. We climbed over the slabs to 'The Sacred Pool'. On our right were groups of spectacular pinnacles and on our left the slabs steepened and curved down out of sight into mist. At the pool Tongal did more mumbo-jumbo and sacrificed one more cockerel; we were getting tired of Tongal and left him to study the entrails while we stumbled over broken boulders to the summit, 300 feet higher.

At the top was a wooden stake painted with Japanese characters. Mist prevented any view down the tremendous eastern precipice into 'Low's Abyss' and we had no view to the west until we were far down the slabs on the descent.

In all, from Paka, I thought we climbed 1500 feet of jungle, 500 feet of slab with moss or scrub and 1500 feet of bare slab. At about 12,500 feet some of us started to race each other for the top and at that height found it utterly exhausting. By the time we got back to the caves Peter and I were tired out and could not at first eat any food.

On 13 February we made our way back from Paka to Bundu Tuhan; it was a long, long way down, but the rain had stopped. We stood out on projecting edges of the ridge feeling like soaring birds above immeasurable depths; the jungle plunged in gigantic steps to the valleys below; there was the coast – Jesselton, Tuaran, and the sea beyond dotted with islands. We paid off the coolies, Labuan and the High Priest, who was troublesome about his stipend.

Bill Darley's section of REME was on the beach near me. He had found that some of the Japs were shipwrights by trade and he got them to make him an 18-foot clinker-built boat with a centre-board. He named her *Samsue* and we sailed her one night to the farthest of the small offshore islands that we could see. I lay on my belly in the bows staring through the clear water at all sizes of jelly-fish, opaque white or delicate mauve in colour. We brought *Samsue* gently to a sandy beach strewn with coral. The sun had just set and the horizon was full of colour and light. Jesselton was faint in the north-east; at hand the palm trees and coral rocks of the islet were silhouetted against the evening sky. The quiet water of the cove into which we had run the boat was clear and green. It was a typical Pacific island and our time ashore was pure delight.

As it grew dark we could not see the mainland well enough to know where to steer and we waited until the lights of our camp began to show, four miles away. Steering by these we ran back with a beam wind, fresh and drawing a little ahead as we went on. The boat was like an animal on the swell, swishing and slapping through the small waves and leaving a steady phosphorescent wake; after a while I steered by the island, gazing astern over the surging wake and singing tonelessly. We landed two hours after sunset, and when I got back to the tents I found a Gurkha with a dislocated shoulder waiting for me.

On 24 February a signal came to my office to say that I was offered 28 days' leave in the UK. I expected to be out of the army in six months or a year, but I accepted; I hoped that after my leave I should come back to 59 Field Ambulance and could then be demobilized in India: I would go to the mountains then. But 59 Field Ambulance was disbanded during my leave and by 1947 India was in the turmoil of 'Partition'.

Tom Wimbush and I travelled luxuriously to Singapore in an empty 'Landing Ship, Tank', with RN Officers. Singapore harbour was full of shipping: troopships, supply ships, and local craft – junks and strange-looking rowing boats with broad sterns from which pieces of wood projected on each quarter. We went ashore at noon in the ship's launch to look for 'Embarkation' and at 1800 we were still waiting on the quay for transport into town. We tackled officers with lorries and officers with jeeps, and always got the same answer: 'Frightfully sorry, old boy, but it's not my *bando* you know.' The quayside smelled of rotting eggs.

At Nee Soon transit camp were two familiar faces from my student days; both had become specialists of some kind and I felt slightly remote from them, a poor relation. The camp was crowded with bored officers trying to move on – reinforcements, leave men and men waiting for repatriation and demobilization. We hired a car and went up to Lombong, a sort of Brighton beach holiday resort where we could scramble about on rocks and bathe under a waterfall in a gorge. We dined at the Tanglin Club and talked about Oxford, now far behind us, and about the future. Another night we took a car to Johore Bahru. Pleasant houses overlooked Johore Strait and we sat out at dining tables on the lawns, looking down on the lights of fishing boats in the Strait. We seemed to be civilians again until, back at Nee Soon, I heard an RSM bark at a sentry, "And get your heels off that brick – another six inches – d'you hear?" Pause. "And take that silly grin off your face."

There was of course no privacy in the camp and we queued for everything, to check in, to check out, to change money; we queued for tea or cocoa and for the beer, which had generally run out by the time you reached the end of the queue; we even queued to eat.

One night as I walked down a passage after dinner I heard a yell and saw a big coal-black figure come running to fling himself on me and give me a tremendous hug; it was Kurup from 7 IMFTU; I had not seen him since Sagaing, near Mandalay, and I was enormously pleased.

Tom Wimbush discovered that war crime trials were being held in Singapore and we made a habit of going along and sitting in the public gallery. They were the trials which became known as the 'Tenth, tenth trials'.

On 10 October, 1943, after explosions which had damaged ships in Johore Strait, the Japanese *kempei tei* had arrested a number of civilians on suspicion of being implicated. The real saboteurs had come boldly by sea and had succeeded in getting away completely in a small boat without getting caught. The *kempei tei* interrogated their luckless captives by torture and some died. It was twenty of these *kempei tei*, under Lieutenant-Colonel Sumida, who were now on trial. The Presiding Officer of the Court was a Lieutenant-Colonel Silkin; the courtroom was crowded with servicemen and civilians. We listened for days with morbid fascination to the witnesses' accounts of what the creatures in the dock had done to them and to those who died. A civilian called Robert Scott gave evidence. He had been brought from England for the purpose and was asked if he recognized any of the people in the dock. At this the Japanese all rose and their colonel gave Scott a formal bow of recognition; a faint smile passed between the two.

'War Crimes Trials' Vol. VIII, edited by Colin Sleeman and S.C. Silkin, records,

"Scott was to withstand the most painful of tortures, the vilest conditions of incarceration and the strongest moral and physical pressure with a gallantry and good humour which the Japanese were quite unable to understand and which probably more than any other factor contributed to the survival of the majority of his fellow prisoners and himself. The same good humour and moderation of outlook and expression Scott later displayed in the witness-box; it will be long before those in court who saw it will forget the smile of greeting which, as Scott went to take the oath, passed between him and Sumida, the principal defendant in the trial, who for months had schemed and battled to break his will. There was no malice between these two – but there was no doubt which of them had been the victor."

Several years later I was able to ask Scott what had helped him not to give in, and he said,

"One thing, you see, was that I knew them, and I knew that if I gave in I should be executed: they would have extracted justification for doing it."

Weakness made us go day after day to listen to horrible details that sickened us for ever of the sight of those Japanese. Several of them, including Colonel Sumida, were hanged; the rest served long prison sentences.

Five months later, after purposeless journeys between the UK and India, I was in a boat, the *Franconia*, that reached Suez at dawn and stayed there until evening. In the morning we reached Port Said, after passing the night at anchor in one of the bitter lakes. On the bows of the ship were searchlights which reached out into the dark: the banks of the canal appeared without end before us. Port Said was the turning point of the voyage for every traveller between the Far East and England. The figure of Ferdinand de Lesseps, later knocked down and destroyed by Nasser, then stood proudly over the harbour. From the anchored ship I could see the start of the canal that he built stretching in a straight line to the horizon and disappearing over the edge of the world. The temperature changed abruptly and serge battledress was ordered to be worn. Bright fresh regimental flashes and medal ribbons appeared, and we eyed each other curiously. In the Western Approaches single boats appeared from every direction and spoke to us, a contrast to the secret convoy travel of our outward voyage over a lonely ocean.

Our landfall was the Bishop Rock Light, Scilly Isles, where we were told that we were going to Liverpool. Two days later we had rounded Bardsey Island and were steaming along the Anglesey coast; it looked fresh and green. The hills beyond were hidden by cloud but those of us who knew that coast could pick out landmarks, Lynas Point where the Liverpool pilot came aboard, Great Orme's Head, the estuary of the Dee and at last the Lancashire coast and the entrance to the Mersey. It began to rain and the evening closed in cold and foggy. We did not leave the ship until next day.

On deck, waiting to go down the gangway, I asked an Indian what his first impression of England was, and he said, "The pall of smoke over Liverpool." A little girl looked over the rail and shouted, "Mummy, Mummy, come here. Look! White men working."

First we were to go to York. I missed the train because of some delay with baggage and long before I reached York the others had gone without ceremony, hurrying on to whatever they expected to find wherever they were going. I toured a drab warehouse full of civilian clothes, and looked for something I could wear: suits, shirts, collars and ties, socks, shoes. The only possible garment was a raincoat not nearly as good as my old belted army 'Raincoat, officers, for the use of'. I helped myself and made my way back to the station with a brown paper parcel; it was all over.

Index